From
A Year With A Whaler

I was awakened suddenly out of a sound sleep in the middle of the night. My friend stood beside my bed with a lighted candle in his hand.

"Get up and come with me," he said. "Don't go whaling. My uncle has told me all about it. He knows. You'll be treated like a dog aboard, fed on rotten grub, and if you don't die under the hard knocks or freeze to death in the Arctic Ocean, you won't get a penny when you get back. Don't be a fool. Take my advice and give that runner the slip. If you go, you'll regret it to the last day of your life."

In the yellow glare of the candle, the young man seemed not unlike an apparition and he delivered his message of warning with prophetic solemnity and impressiveness. But my mind was made up.

"I guess I'll go," I said.

A YEAR WITH A
WHALER

A YEAR WITH A
WHALER

WALTER NOBLE BURNS

Warwick, NY

CONTENTS

1

The Lure of the Outfitter

WHEN the brig *Alexander* sailed out of San Francisco on a whaling voyage a few years ago, I was a member of her forecastle crew. Once outside the Golden Gate, I felt the swing of blue water under me for the first time in my life. I was not shanghaied. Let's have that settled at the start. I had shipped as a green hand before the mast for the adventure of the thing, because I wanted to go, for the glamour of the sea was upon me.

I was taking breakfast in a San Francisco restaurant when, in glancing over the morning paper, I chanced across this advertisement:

> Wanted—Men for a whaling voyage; able seamen, ordinary seamen, and green hands. No experience necessary. Big money for a lucky voyage. Apply at Levy's, No. 12 Washington Street.

Until that moment I had never dreamed of going to sea, but that small "ad" laid its spell upon my imagination. It was big with the lure of strange lands and climes, romance and fresh experiences. What did it matter that I had passed all my humdrum days on dry land? "No experience necessary!" There were the magic words staring me in the face. I gulped down my eggs and coffee and was off for the street called Washington.

Levy's was a ship's outfitting store. A "runner" for the house—a hulking man with crafty eyes and a face almost as red as his hair and mustache—met me as I stepped in the door. He looked me over critically. His visual inventory must have been satisfactory. I was young.

"Ever been a sailor?" he asked.

"No."

"Makes no difference. Can you pull an oar?"

"Yes."

"You'll do. Hang around the store to-day and I'll see what vessels are shipping crews."

That was all. I was a potential whaler from that minute.

A young working man in overalls and flannel shirt came in later in the day and applied to go on the voyage. He qualified as a green hand. But no spirit of adventure had brought him to

Levy's. A whaling voyage appealed to his canny mind as a business proposition.

"What can we make?" he asked the runner.

"If your ship is lucky," replied the runner, "you ought to clean up a pile of money. You'll ship on the 190th lay. Know what a lay is? It's your per cent of the profits of the voyage. Say your ship catches four whales. She ought to catch a dozen if she has good luck. But say she catches four. Her cargo in oil and bone will be worth about $50,000. Your share will amount to something like $200, and you'll get it in a lump sum when you get back."

This was "bunk talk"—a "springe to catch woodcock"—but we did not know it. That fluent and plausible man took pencil and paper and showed us just how it would all work out. It was reserved for us poor greenhorns to learn later on that sailors of whaling ships usually are paid off at the end of a voyage with "one big iron dollar." This fact being discreetly withheld from us, our illusions were not disturbed.

The fact is the "lay" means nothing to sailors on a whaler. It is merely a lure for the unsophisticated. It might as well be the 1000th lay as the 190th, for all the poor devil of a sailor gets. The explanation is simple. The men start the voyage with an insufficient supply of clothing. By the time the vessel strikes cold weather their clothes are worn out and it is a case of buy clothes from the ship's slop-chest at the captain's own prices or freeze. As a consequence, the men come back to port with expense accounts standing against them which wipe out all possible profits. This has become so definitely a part of whaling custom that no sailor ever thinks of fighting against it and it probably would do him no good if he did. As a forecastle hand's pay the "big iron dollar" is a whaling tradition and as fixed and inevitable as fate.

The outfitter who owned the store did not conduct a sailor's boarding house, so we were put up at a cheap hotel on Pacific Street. After supper, my new friend took me for a visit to the home of his uncle in the Tar Flats region. A rough, kindly old laboring man was this uncle who sat in his snug parlor in his shirt sleeves during our stay, sent one of the children to the corner for a growler of beer, and told us bluntly we were idiots to think of shipping on a whaling voyage. We laughed at his warning—we were going and that's all there was to it. The old fellow's pretty daughters played the piano and sang for us, and my last evening on shore passed pleasantly enough. When it came time to say goodbye, the uncle prevailed on my friend to stay all night on the plea that he had some urgent matters to talk over, and I went back alone to my dingy hotel on the Barbary Coast.

I was awakened suddenly out of a sound sleep in the middle of the night. My friend stood beside my bed with a lighted candle in his hand.

"Get up and come with me," he said. "Don't go whaling. My uncle has told me all about it. He knows. You'll be treated like a dog aboard, fed on rotten grub, and if you don't die under the hard knocks or freeze to death in the Arctic Ocean, you won't get a penny when you get back. Don't be a fool. Take my advice and give that runner the slip. If you go, you'll regret it to the last day of your life."

In the yellow glare of the candle, the young man seemed not unlike an apparition and he delivered his message of warning with prophetic solemnity and impressiveness. But my mind was made up.

"I guess I'll go," I said.

He argued and pleaded with me, all to no purpose. He set the candle on the table and blew it out.

"You won't come?" he said out of the darkness.

"No."

"You're a fool."

He slammed the door. I never saw him again. But many a time on the long voyage I recalled his wise counsel, prompted as it was by pure friendliness, and wished from my heart I had taken his advice.

Next day the runner for Levy's tried to ship me aboard the steam whaler *William Lewis*. When we arrived at the shipping office on the water front, it was crowded with sailors and rough fellows, many of them half drunk, and all eager for a chance to land a berth. A bronzed and bearded man stood beside a desk and surveyed them. He was the skipper of the steamer. The men were pushing and elbowing in an effort to get to the front and catch his eye.

"I've been north before, captain," "I'm an able seaman, sir," "I know the ropes," "Give me a chance, captain," "Take me, sir; I'll make a good hand,"—so they clamored their virtues noisily. The captain chose this man and that. In twenty minutes his crew was signed. It was not a question of getting enough men; it was a mere matter of selection. In such a crowd of sailormen, I stood no show. In looking back on it all, I wonder how such shipping office scenes are possible, how men of ordinary intelligence are herded aboard whale ships like sheep, how they even fight for a chance to go.

It was just as well I failed to ship aboard the *William Lewis*. The vessel went to pieces in the ice on the north Alaskan coast the following spring. Four men lost their lives and only after a bitter experience as castaways on the floes were the others rescued.

That afternoon Captain Shorey of the brig *Alexander* visited Levy's. I was called to his attention as a likely young hand and he shipped me as a member of his crew. I signed articles for a year's voyage. It was provided that I was to receive a $50 advance with which to outfit myself for the voyage; of course, any money left over after all necessary articles had been purchased was to be mine—at least, in my innocence, I imagined it was.

The brig was lying in the stream off Goat Island and the runner set about the work of outfitting me at once. He and I and a clerk went about the store from shelf to shelf, selecting articles. The runner carried a pad of paper on which he marked down the cost. I was given a sailor's canvas bag, a mattress, a pair of blankets, woolen trousers, dungaree trousers, a coat, a pair of brogans, a pair of rubber sea boots, underwear, socks, two flannel shirts, a cap, a belt and sheath knife, a suit of oil-skins and sou'wester, a tin cup, tin pan, knife, fork and spoon. That was all.

It struck me as a rather slender equipment for a year's voyage. The runner footed up the cost.

"Why," he said with an air of great surprise, "this foots up to $53 and your advance is only $50."

He added up the column of figures again. But he had made no mistake. He seemed perplexed.

"I don't see how it is possible to scratch off anything," he said. "You'll need every one of these articles."

He puckered his brow, bit the end of his pencil, and studied the figures. It was evidently a puzzling problem.

"Well," he said at last, "I'll tell you what I'll do. Bring me down a few curios from the Arctic and I'll call it square."

I suppose my outfit was really worth about $6—not over $10. As soon as my bag had been packed, I was escorted to the wharf by the runner and rowed out to the brig. As I prepared to climb over the ship's rail, the runner shook me by the hand and clapped me on the back with a great show of cordial good fellowship.

"Don't forget my curios," he said.

2

The Men of the
"Alexander"

THE brig *Alexander* was a staunch, seaworthy little vessel. She had no fine lines; there was nothing about her to please a yachtsman's eye; but she was far from being a tub as whaling ships are often pictured. She was built at New Bedford especially for Arctic whaling. Her hull was of sturdy oak, reinforced at the bows to enable her to buck her way through ice.

Though she was called a brig, she was really a brigantine, rigged with square sails on her fore-mast and with fore-and-aft sails on her main. She was of only 128 tons but quite lofty, her royal yard being eighty feet above the deck. On her fore-mast she carried a fore-sail, a single topsail, a fore-top-gallant sail, and a royal; on her main-mast, a big mainsail with a gaff-topsail above it. Three whale boats—starboard, larboard, and waist boats—hung at her davits. Amidships stood the brick try-works equipped with furnaces and cauldrons for rendering blubber into oil.

As soon as I arrived on board I was taken in charge by the ship keeper and conducted to the forecastle. It was a dark, malodorous, triangular hole below the deck in the bows. At the foot of the ladder-like stairs, leading down through the scuttle, I stepped on something soft and yielding. Was it possible, I wondered in an instant's flash of surprise, that the forecastle was laid with a velvet carpet? No, it was not. It was only a Kanaka sailor lying on the floor dead drunk.

The bunks were ranged round the walls in a double tier. I selected one for myself, arranged my mattress and blankets, and threw my bag inside. I was glad to get back to fresh air on deck as quickly as possible.

Members of the crew kept coming aboard in charge of runners and boarding bosses. They were a hard looking lot; several were staggering drunk, and most of them were tipsy. All had bottles and demijohns of whiskey. Everybody was full of bad liquor and high spirits that first night on the brig. A company of jolly sea rovers were we, and we joked and laughed and roared out songs like so many pirates about to cruise for treasure galleons on the Spanish Main. Somehow next morning the rose color had faded out of the prospect and there were many aching heads aboard.

On the morning of the second day, the officers came out to the vessel. A tug puffed alongside and made fast to us with a cable. The anchor was heaved up and, with the tug towing us, we headed for the Golden Gate. Outside the harbor heads, the tug cast loose and put back into the bay in a cloud of smoke. The brig was left swinging on the long swells of the Pacific.

The captain stopped pacing up and down the quarter-deck and said something to the mate. His words seemed like a match to powder. Immediately the mate began roaring out orders. Boat-steerers bounded forward, shouting out the orders in turn. The old sailors sang them out in repetition. Men sprang aloft. Loosened sails were soon rolling down and fluttering from every spar. The sailors began pulling on halyards and yo-hoing on sheets. Throughout the work of setting sail, the green hands were "at sea" in a double sense. The bustle and apparent confusion of the scene seemed to savor of bedlam broke loose. The orders were Greek to them. They stood about, bewildered and helpless. Whenever they tried to help the sailors they invariably snarled things up and were roundly abused for their pains. One might fancy they could at least have helped pull on a rope. They couldn't even do that. Pulling on a rope, sailor-fashion, is in itself an art.

Finally all the sails were sheeted home. Ropes were coiled up and hung neatly on belaying pins. A fresh breeze set all the snowy canvas drawing and the brig, all snug and shipshape, went careering southward.

At the outset of the voyage, the crew consisted of twenty-four men. Fourteen men were in the forecastle. The after-crew comprised the captain, mate, second mate, third mate, two boat-steerers, steward, cooper, cook, and cabin boy. Captain Shorey was not aboard. He was to join the vessel at Honolulu. Mr. Winchester, the mate, took the brig to the Hawaiian Islands as captain. This necessitated a graduated rise in authority all along the line. Mr. Landers, who had shipped as second mate, became mate; Gabriel, the regular third mate, became second mate; and Mendez, a boat-steerer, was advanced to the position of third mate.

Captain Winchester was a tall, spare, vigorous man with a nose like Julius Caesar's and a cavernous bass voice that boomed like a sunset gun. He was a man of some education, which is a rarity among officers of whale ships, and was a typical New England Yankee. He had run away to sea as a boy and had been engaged in the whaling trade for twenty years. For thirteen years, he had been sailing to the Arctic Ocean as master and mate of vessels, and was ingrained with the autocratic traditions of the quarter-deck. Though every inch a sea dog of the hard, old-fashioned school, he had his kindly human side, as I learned later. He was by far the best whaleman aboard the brig; as skillful and daring as any that ever laid a boat on a whale's back; a fine, bold, hardy type of seaman and an honor to the best traditions of the sea. He lost his life—poor fellow—in a whaling adventure in the Arctic Ocean on his next voyage.

Mr. Landers, the mate, was verging on sixty; his beard was grizzled, but there wasn't a streak of gray in his coal-black hair. He was stout and heavy-limbed and must have been remarkably strong in his youth. He was a Cape Codder and talked with a quaint, nasal, Yankee drawl. He had been to sea all his life and was a whaleman of thirty years experience. In all these years, he had been ashore very little—only a few weeks between his year-long voyages, during which time, it was said, he kept up his preference for liquids, exchanging blue water for red liquor.

He was a picturesque old fellow, and was so accustomed to the swinging deck of a ship under him that standing or sitting, in perfectly still weather or with the vessel lying motionless at anchor, he swayed his body from side to side heavily as if in answer to the rise and fall of waves. He was a silent, easy-going man, with a fund of dry humor and hard common sense. He never did any more work than he had to, and before the voyage ended, he was suspected by the officers of being a malingerer. All the sailors liked him.

Gabriel, the second mate, was a Negro from the Cape Verde islands. His native language was Portuguese and he talked funny, broken English. He was about forty-five years old, and though he was almost as dark-skinned as any Ethiopian, he had hair and a full beard as finely spun and free from kinkiness as a Caucasian's. The sailors used to say that Gabriel was a white man born black by accident. He was a kindly, cheerful soul with shrewd native wit. He was a whaleman of life-long experience.

Mendez, the third mate, and Long John, one of the boat-steerers, were also Cape Verde islanders. Long John was a giant, standing six feet, four inches; an ungainly, powerful fellow, with a black face as big as a ham and not much more expressive. He had the reputation of being one of the most expert harpooners of the Arctic Ocean whaling fleet.

Little Johnny, the other boat-steerer, was a mulatto from the Barbados, English islands of the West Indies. He was a strapping, intelligent young man, brimming over with vitality and high spirits and with all a plantation darky's love of fun. His eyes were bright and his cheeks ruddy with perfect health; he loved dress and gay colors and was quite the dandy of the crew.

Five of the men of the forecastle were deep-water sailors. Of these one was an American, one a German, one a Norwegian, and two Swedes. They followed the sea for a living and had been bunkoed by their boarding bosses into believing they would make large sums of money whaling. They had been taken in by a confidence game as artfully as the man who loses his money at the immemorial trick of three shells and a pea. When they learned they would get only a dollar at the end of the voyage and contemplated the loss of an entire working year, they were full of resentment and righteous, though futile, anger.

Taylor, the American, became the acknowledged leader of the forecastle. He quickly established himself in this position, not only by his skill and long experience as a seaman, but by his aggressiveness, his domineering character, and his physical ability to deal with men and situations. He was a bold, iron-fisted fellow to whom the green hands looked for instruction and advice, whom several secretly feared, and for whom all had a wholesome respect.

Nels Nelson, a red-haired, red-bearded old Swede, was the best sailor aboard. He had had a thousand adventures on all the seas of all the world. He had been around Cape Horn seven times—a sailor is not rated as a really-truly sailor until he has made a passage around that stormy promontory—and he had rounded the Cape of Good Hope so many times he had lost the count. He had ridden out a typhoon on the coast of Japan and had been driven ashore by a hurricane in the West Indies. He had sailed on an expedition to Cocos Island, that realm of mystery and romance, to try to lift pirate treasure in doubloons, plate, and pieces-of-eight, supposed to have been buried there by "Bugs" Thompson and Benito Bonito, those one-time terrors of the Spanish Main. He had been cast away in the South Seas in an open boat with three companions, and had eaten the flesh of the man whose fate had been sealed by the casting of lots. He was some man, was Nelson. I sometimes vaguely suspected he was some liar, too, but I don't know, I think most of his stories were true.

He could do deftly everything intricate and subtle in sailorcraft from tying the most wonderful knots to splicing wire. None of the officers could teach old Nelson anything about fancy sailorizing and they knew it. Whenever they wanted an unusual or particularly difficult piece of work done they called on him, and he always did it in the best seamanly fashion.

Richard, the German, was a sturdy, manly young chap who had served in the German navy. He was well educated and a smart seaman. Ole Oleson, the Norwegian, was just out of his teens but a fine sailor. Peter Swenson, a Swede, was a chubby, rosy boy of sixteen, an ignorant, reckless, devil-may-care lad, who was looked upon as the baby of the forecastle and humored and spoiled accordingly.

Among the six white green hands, there was a "mule skinner" from western railway construction camps; a cowboy who believed himself fitted for the sea after years of experience on the "hurricane deck" of a bucking bronco; a country boy straight from the plow and with "farmer" stamped all over him in letters of light; a man suspected of having had trouble with the police; another who, in lazy night watches, spun frank yarns of burglaries; and "Slim," an Irishman who said he had served with the Royal Life Guards in the English army. There was one old whaler. He was a shiftless, loquacious product of city slums. This was his seventh whaling voyage—which would seem sufficient comment on his character.

"It beats hoboing," he said. And as his life's ambition seemed centered on three meals a day and a bunk to sleep in, perhaps it did.

Two Kanakas completed the forecastle crew, these and the cabin boy, who was also a Kanaka, talked fair English, but among themselves they always spoke their native language. I had heard much of the liquid beauty of the Kanaka tongue. It was a surprise to find it the most unmusical and harshly guttural language I ever heard. It comes from the mouth in a series of explosive grunts and gibberings. The listener is distinctly and painfully impressed with the idea that if the nitroglycerine words were retained in the system, they would prove dangerous to health and is fearful lest they choke the spluttering Kanaka to death before he succeeds in biting them off and flinging them into the atmosphere.

3

Why We Don't Desert

A S soon as we were under sail, the crew was called aft and the watches selected. Gabriel was to head the starboard watch and Mendez the port. The men were ranged in line and the heads of the watches made their selections, turn and turn about. The deep-water sailors were the first to be chosen. The green hands were picked for their appearance of strength and activity. I fell into the port watch.

Sea watches were now set—four hours for sleep and four for work throughout the twenty-four. My watch was sent below. No one slept during this first watch below, but we made up for lost time during our second turn. Soon we became accustomed to the routine and found it as restful as the usual landsman's method of eight hours sleep and sixteen of wakefulness.

It is difficult for a landlubber to understand how sailors on shipboard can be kept constantly busy. The brig was a veritable hive of industry. The watch on deck when morning broke pumped ship and swept and flushed down the decks. During the day watches, in addition to working the ship, we were continuously breaking out supplies, keeping the water barrel on deck filled from casks in the hold, laboring with the cargo, scrubbing paint work, polishing brass work, slushing masts and spars, repairing rigging, and attending to a hundred and one details that must be looked after every day. The captain of a ship is one of the most scrupulous housekeepers in the world and only by keeping his crew busy from morning till night is he able to keep his ship spick and span and in proper repair. Whale ships are supposed to be dirty. On the contrary, they are kept as clean as water and brooms and hard work can keep them.

The food served aboard the brig was nothing to brag about. Breakfast consisted of corned-beef hash, hardtack, and coffee without milk or sugar. We sweetened our coffee with molasses, a keg of which was kept in the forecastle. For dinner, we had soup, corned-beef stew, called "skouse," a loaf of soft bread, and coffee. For supper, we had slices of corned-beef which the sailors called "salt horse," hardtack, and tea. The principal variation in this diet was in the soups.

The days were a round of barley soup, bean soup, pea soup, and back to barley soup again, an alternation that led the men to speak of the days of the week not as Monday, Tuesday, and so on, but as "barley soup day," "bean soup day," and "pea soup day." Once or twice a week we had gingerbread for supper. On the other hand the cabin fared sumptuously on canned vegetables, meat, salmon, soft bread, tea, and coffee with sugar and condensed milk, fresh fish and meat whenever procurable, and a dessert every day at dinner, including plum duff, a famous sea delicacy which never in all the voyage found its way forward.

From the first day, the green hands were set learning the ropes, to stand lookout, to take their trick at the wheel, to reef and furl and work among the sails. These things are the ABC of seamanship, but they are not to be learned in a day or a week. A ship is a complicated mechanism, and it takes a long time for a novice to acquire even the rudiments of sea education. Going aloft was a terrifying ordeal at first to several of the green hands, though it never bothered me.

When the cowboy was first ordered to furl the fore-royal, he hung back and said, "I can't" and "I'll fall," and whimpered and begged to be let off. But he was forced to try. He climbed the ratlines slowly and painfully to the royal yard, and he finally furled the sail, though it took him a long time to do it. He felt so elated that after that he wanted to furl the royal every time it had to be done—didn't want to give anyone else a chance.

Furling the royal was a one-man job. The foot-rope was only a few feet below the yard, and if a man stood straight on it, the yard would strike him a little above the knees. If the ship were pitching, a fellow had to look sharp or he would be thrown off—if that had happened it was a nice straight fall of eighty feet to the deck. My own first experience on the royal yard gave me an exciting fifteen minutes. The ship seemed to be fighting me and devoting an unpleasant amount of time and effort to it; bucking and tossing as if with a sentient determination to shake me off into the atmosphere. I escaped becoming a grease spot on the deck of the brig only by hugging the yard as if it were a sweetheart and hanging on for dear life. I became in time quite an expert at furling the sail.

Standing lookout was the one thing aboard a green hand could do as well as an old sailor.

The lookout was posted on the forecastle head in fair weather and on the try-works in a storm. He stood two hours at a stretch. He had to scan the sea ahead closely and if a sail or anything unusual appeared, he reported to the officer of the watch.

Learning to steer by the compass was comparatively easy. With the ship heading on a course, it was not difficult by manipulating the wheel to keep the needle of the compass on a given point. But to steer by the wind was hard to learn and is sometimes a nice matter even for skillful seamen. When a ship is close-hauled and sailing, as sailors say, right in the wind's eye, the wind is blowing into the braced sails at the weather edge of the canvas—if the vessel were brought any higher up, the wind would pour around on the back of the sails. The helmsman's aim is to keep the luff of the royal sail or of the sails that happen to be set, wrinkling and loose—luffing, sailors call it. That shows that the wind is slanting into the sails at just the right angle and perhaps a little bit is spilling over.

I gradually learned to do this in the daytime. But at night when it was almost impossible for me to see the luff of the sails clearly, it was extremely difficult and I got into trouble more than once by my clumsiness. The trick at the wheel was of two hours duration.

The second day out from San Francisco was Christmas. I had often read that Christmas was a season of good cheer and happiness among sailors at sea, that it was commemorated with religious service, and that the skipper sent forward grog and plum duff to gladden the hearts of the sailormen. But Santa Claus forgot the sailors on the brig. Bean soup only distinguished Christmas from the day that had gone before and the day that came after. No liquor or tempting dishes came to the forecastle. It was the usual day of hard work from dawn to dark.

After two weeks of variable weather during which we were often becalmed, we put into Turtle Bay, midway down the coast of lower California, and dropped anchor.

Turtle Bay is a beautiful little land-locked harbor on an uninhabited coast. There was no village or any human habitation on its shores. A desolate, treeless country, seamed by gullies and scantily covered with sun-dried grass, rolled away to a chain of high mountains which forms the backbone of the peninsula of lower California. These mountains were perhaps thirty miles from the coast; they were gray and apparently barren of trees or any sort of herbage, and looked to be ridges of naked granite. The desert character of the landscape was a surprise, as we were almost within the tropics.

We spent three weeks of hard work in Turtle Bay. Sea watches were abolished and all hands were called on deck at dawn and kept busy until sundown. The experienced sailors were employed as sail makers; squatting all day on the quarter-deck, sewing on canvas with a palm and needle. Old sails were sent down from the spars and patched and repaired. If they were too far gone, new sails were bent in their stead.

The green hands had the hard work. They broke out the hold and restowed every piece of cargo, arranging it so that the vessel rode on a perfectly even keel. Yards and masts were slushed, the rigging was tarred, and the ship was painted inside and out.

The waters of the harbor were alive with Spanish mackerel, albacore, rock bass, bonitos, and other kinds of fish. The mackerel appeared in great schools that rippled the water as if a strong breeze were blowing. These fish attracted great numbers of gray pelicans, which had the most wonderful mode of flight I have ever seen in any bird. For hours at a time, with perfectly motionless pinions, they skimmed the surface of the bay like living aeroplanes; one wondered wherein lay their motor power and how they managed to keep going. When they spied a school of mackerel, they rose straight into the air with a great flapping of wings, then turned their heads downward, folded their wings close to their bodies, and dropped like a stone. Their great beaks cut the water; they went under with a terrific splash, and immediately emerged with a fish in the net-like membrane beneath their lower mandible.

Every Sunday, a boat's crew went fishing. We fished with hand lines weighted with lead and having three or four hooks, baited at first with bacon and later with pieces of fresh fish. I never had such fine fishing. The fish bit as fast as we could throw in our lines, and we were kept busy hauling them out of the water. We would fill a whale boat almost to the gunwales in a few hours. With the return of the first fishing expedition, the sailors had dreams of a feast, but they were disappointed. The fish went to the captain's table or were salted away in barrels for the cabin's future use. The sailors, however, enjoyed the fun. Many of them kept lines constantly over the brig's sides, catching skates, soles, and little sharks.

By the time we reached Turtle Bay, it was no longer a secret that we would get only a dollar for our year's voyage. As a result, a feverish spirit of discontent began to manifest itself among those forward and plans to run away became rife. We were anchored about a half mile from shore, and after looking over the situation, I made up my mind to try to escape. Except for an officer and a boat-steerer who stood watch, all hands were asleep below at night. Being a good swimmer, I planned to slip over the bow in the darkness and swim ashore. Once on land, I figured it would be an easy matter to cross the Sierras and reach a Mexican settlement on the Gulf of California.

Possibly the officers got wind of the runaway plots brewing in the forecastle, for Captain Winchester came forward one evening, something he never had done before, and fell into gossipy talk with the men.

"Have you noticed that pile of stones with a cross sticking in it on the harbor head?" he asked in a casual sort of way.

Yes, we had all noticed it from the moment we dropped anchor, and had wondered what it was.

"That," said the captain impressively, "is a grave. Whaling vessels have been coming to Turtle Bay for years to paint ship and overhaul. Three sailors on a whaler several years ago thought this was a likely place in which to escape. They managed to swim ashore at night and struck into the hills. They expected to find farms and villages back inland. They didn't know that the whole peninsula of lower California is a waterless desert from one end to the other. They had some food with them and they kept going for days. No one knows how far inland they traveled, but they found neither inhabitants nor water and their food was soon gone.

"When they couldn't stand it any longer and were half dying from thirst and hunger, they turned back for the coast. By the time they returned to Turtle Bay their ship had sailed away and there they were on a desert shore without food or water and no way to get either. I suppose they camped on the headland in the hope of hailing a passing ship. But the vessels that pass up and down this coast usually keep out of sight of land. Maybe the poor devils sighted a distant topsail—no one knows—but if they did the ship sank beyond the horizon without paying any attention to their frantic signals. So they died miserably there on the headland.

"Next year, a whale ship found their bodies and erected a cairn of stones marked by the cross you see over the spot where the three sailors were buried together. This is a bad country to run away in," the captain added. "No food, no water, no inhabitants. It's sure death for a runaway."

Having spun this tragic yarn, Captain Winchester went aft again, feeling, no doubt, that he had sowed seed on fertile soil. The fact is his story had an instant effect. Most of the men abandoned their plans to escape, at least for the time being, hoping a more favorable opportunity would present itself when we reached the Hawaiian Islands. But I had my doubts. I thought it possible the captain merely had put over a good bluff.

Next day I asked Little Johnny, the boat-steerer, if it were true as the captain had said that lower California was an uninhabited desert. He assured me it was and to prove it, he brought out a ship's chart from the cabin and spread it before me. I found that only two towns throughout the length and breadth of the peninsula were set down on the map. One of these was Tijuana on the west coast just south of the United States boundary line and the other was La Paz on the east coast near Cape St. Lucas, the southern tip of the peninsula. Turtle Bay was two or three hundred miles from either town.

That settled it with me. I didn't propose to take chances on dying in the desert. I preferred a whaler's forecastle to that.

4

Turtles and Porpoises

WE shipped out of Turtle Bay one moonlight night and stood southward. We were now in sperm whale waters and the crews of the whale boats were selected. Captain Winchester was to head the starboard boat; Mr. Landers the larboard boat; and Gabriel the waist boat. Long John was to act as boat-steerer for Mr. Winchester, Little Johnny for Mr. Landers, and Mendez for Gabriel. The whale boats were about twenty-five feet long, rigged with leg-of-mutton sails and jibs. The crew of each consisted of an officer known as a boat-header, who sat in the stern and wielded the tiller; a boat-steerer or harpooner, whose position was in the bow; and four sailors who pulled the stroke, midship, tub, and bow oars. Each boat had a tub in which four hundred fathoms of whale line were coiled and carried two harpoons and a shoulder bomb-gun. I was assigned to the midship oar of Gabriel's boat.

Let me take occasion just here to correct a false impression quite generally held regarding whaling. Many persons—I think, most persons—have an idea that in modern whaling, harpoons are fired at whales from the decks of ships. This is true only of long-shore whaling. In this trade, fin-backs and the less valuable varieties of whales are chased by small steamers which fire harpoons from guns in the bows and tow the whales they kill to factories along shore, where blubber, flesh, and skeleton are turned into commercial products. Many published articles have familiarized the public with this method of whaling.

But whaling on the sperm grounds of the tropics and on the right whale and bowhead grounds of the polar seas is much the same as it has always been. Boats still go on the backs of whales. Harpoons are thrown by hand into the great animals as of yore. Whales still run away with the boats, pulling them with amazing speed through walls of split water. Whales still crush boats with blows of their mighty flukes and spill their crews into the sea.

There is just as much danger and just as much thrill and excitement in the whaling of to-day as there was in that of a century ago. Neither steamers nor sailing vessels that cruise for sperm and bowhead and right whales nowadays have deck guns of any sort, but depend entirely upon the bomb-guns attached to harpoons and upon shoulder bomb-guns wielded from the whale boats.

In the old days, after whales had been harpooned, they were stabbed to death with long, razor-sharp lances. The lance is a thing of the past. The tonite bomb has taken its place as an instrument of destruction. In the use of the tonite bomb lies the chief difference between modern whaling and the whaling of the old school.

The modern harpoon is the same as it has been since the palmy days of the old South Sea sperm fisheries. But fastened on its iron shaft between the wooden handle and the spear point is a brass cylinder an inch in diameter, perhaps, and about a foot long. This cylinder is a tonite bomb-gun. A short piece of metal projects from the flat lower end. This is the trigger. When the harpoon is thrown into the buttery, blubber-wrapped body of the whale, it sinks in until the whale's skin presses the trigger up into the gun and fires it with a tiny sound like the explosion of an old-fashioned shotgun cap. An instant later a tonite bomb explodes with a muffled roar in the whale's vitals.

The Arctic Ocean whaling fleet which sails out of San Francisco and which in the year of my voyage numbered thirty vessels makes its spring rendezvous in the Hawaiian Islands. Most of the ships leave San Francisco in December and reach Honolulu in March. The two or three months spent in this leisurely voyage are known in whaler parlance as "between seasons." On the way to the islands the ships cruise for sperm whales and sometimes lower for finbacks, sulphur-bottoms, California grays, and even blackfish, to practice their green hand crews.

Captain Winchester did not care particularly whether he took any sperm whales or not, though sperm oil is still valuable. The brig was not merely a blubber-hunter. Her hold was filled with oil tanks which it was hoped would be filled before we got back, but the chief purpose of the voyage was the capture of right and bowhead whales—the great baleen whales of the North.

As soon as we left Turtle Bay, a lookout for whales was posted. During the day watches, a boat-steerer and a sailor sat on the topsail yard for two hours at a stretch and scanned the sea for spouts. We stood down the coast of lower California and in a few days, were in the tide-rip which is always running off Cape St.

Lucas, where the waters of the Pacific meet a counter-current from the Gulf of California. We rounded Cape St. Lucas and sailed north into the gulf, having a distant view of La Paz, a little town backed by gray mountains. Soon we turned south again, keeping close to the Mexican coast for several days. I never learned how far south we went, but we must have worked pretty well toward the equator, for when we stood out across the Pacific for the Hawaiian Islands, our course was northwesterly.

I saw my first whales one morning while working in the bows with the watch under Mr. Landers's supervision. A school of finbacks was out ahead moving in leisurely fashion toward the brig. There were about twenty of them and the sea was dotted with their fountains.

"Blow!" breathed old man Landers with mild interest as though to himself.

"Blow!" boomed Captain Winchester in his big bass voice from the quarter-deck.

"Nothin' but finbacks, sir," shouted the boat-steerer from the mast-head.

"All right," sang back the captain. "Let 'em blow."

It was easy for these old whalers even at this distance to tell they were not sperm whales. Their fountains rose straight into the air. A sperm whale's spout slants up from the water diagonally.

The whales were soon all about the ship, seemingly unafraid, still traveling leisurely, their heads rising and falling rhythmically, and at each rise blowing up a fountain of mist fifteen feet high. The fountains looked like water; some water surely was mixed with them; but I was told that the mist was the breath of the animals made visible by the colder air. The breath came from the blow holes in a sibilant roar that resembled no sound I had ever heard. If one can imagine a giant of fable snoring in his sleep, one may have an idea of the sound of the mighty exhalation. The great lungs whose gentle breathing could shoot a jet of spray fifteen feet into the air must have had the power of enormous bellows.

Immense coal-black fellows these finbacks were—some at least sixty or seventy feet long. One swam so close to the brig that when he blew, the spray fell all about me, wetting my clothes like dew. The finback is a baleen whale and a cousin of the right whale and the bowhead. Their mouths are edged with close-set slabs of baleen, which, however, is so short that it is worthless for commercial purposes. They are of much slenderer build than the more valuable species of whale. Their quickness and activity make them dangerous when hunted in the boats, but their bodies are encased in blubber so thin that it is as worthless as their bone. Consequently they are not hunted unless a whaling ship is hard up for oil.

We gradually worked into the trade winds that blew steadily from the southeast. These winds stayed with us for several weeks or rather we stayed with the winds; while in them it was rarely necessary to take in or set a sail or brace a yard. After we had passed through these aerial rivers, flowing through definite, if invisible, banks, we struck the doldrums—areas of calm between wind currents—they might be called whirlpools of stillness. Later in the day light, fitful breezes finally pushed us through them into the region of winds again.

The slow voyage to the Hawaiian Islands— on the sperm whale grounds, we cruised under short sail—might have proved monotonous if we had not been kept constantly busy and if diverting incidents had not occurred almost every day. Once we sighted three immense turtles sunning themselves on the sea. To the captain they held out prospect of soups and delicate dishes for the cabin table, and with Long John as boat-steerer, a boat was lowered for them. I expected it would be difficult to get within darting distance. What was my surprise to see the turtles, with heads in the air and perfectly aware of their danger, remain upon the surface until the boat was directly upon them. The fact was they could not go under quickly; the big shells kept them afloat. Long John dropped his harpoon crashing through the shell of one of the turtles, flopped it into the boat, and then went on without particular hurry, and captured the other two in the same way. The cabin feasted for several days on the delicate flesh of the turtles; the forecastle got only a savory smell from the galley, as was usual.

We ran into a school of porpoises on another occasion—hundreds of them rolling and tumbling about the ship, like fat porkers on a frolic. Little Johnny took a position on the forecastle head with a harpoon, the line from which had been made fast to the fore-bitt. As a porpoise rose beneath him, he darted his harpoon straight into its back. The sea pig went wriggling under, leaving the water dyed with its blood. It was hauled aboard, squirming and twisting. Little Johnny harpooned two more before the school took fright and disappeared. The porpoises were cleaned and some of their meat, nicely roasted, was sent to the forecastle. It made fine eating, tasting something like beef.

The steward was an inveterate fisherman and constantly kept a baited hook trailing in the brig's wake, the line tied to the taff-rail. He caught a great many bonitos and one day landed a dolphin. We had seen many of these beautiful fish swimming about the ship—long, graceful and looking like an animate streak of blue sky. The steward's dolphin was about five feet long. I had often seen in print the statement that dolphins turned all colors of the rainbow in dying and I had as often seen the assertion branded as a mere figment of poetic imagination. Our dolphin proved the truth of the poetic tradition. As life departed, it changed from blue to green, bronze, salmon, gold, and gray, making death as beautiful as a gorgeous kaleidoscope.

We saw flying fish every day—great "coveys" of them, one may say. They frequently flew several hundred yards, fluttering their webbed side fins like the wings of a bird, sometimes rising fifteen to twenty feet above the water, and curving and zigzagging in their flight. More than once they flew directly across the ship and several fell on deck.

I was talking with Kaiuli, the Kanaka, one night when we heard a soft little thud on deck. I should have paid no attention but Kaiuli was alert on the instant.

"Flying feesh," he cried zestfully and rushed off to search the deck. He found the fish and ate it raw, smacking his lips over it with great gusto. The Hawaiian Islanders, he told me, esteem raw flying fish a great delicacy.

I never saw water so "darkly, deeply, beautifully blue" as in the middle of the Pacific where we had some four miles of water under us. It was as blue as indigo. At night, the sea seemed afire with riotous phosphorescence. White flames leaped about the bows where the brig cut the water before a fresh breeze; the wake was a broad, glowing path. When white caps were running every wave broke in sparks and tongues of flame, and the ocean presented the appearance of a prairie swept by fire. A big shark came swimming about the ship one night and it shone like a living incandescence—a silent, ghost-like shape slowly gliding under the brig and out again.

The idle night watches in the tropics were great times for story telling. The deep-water sailors were especially fond of this way of passing the time. While the green hands were engaging in desultory talk and wishing for the bell to strike to go back to their bunks, these deep-water fellows would be pacing up and down or sitting on deck against the bulwarks, smoking their pipes and spinning yarns to each other. The stories as a rule were interminable and were full of "Then he says" and "Then the other fellow says." It was a poor story that did not last out a four-hour watch and many of them were regular "continued in our next" serials, being cut short at the end of one watch to be resumed in the next.

No matter how long-winded or prosy the narrative, the story teller was always sure of an audience whose attention never flagged for an instant. The boyish delight of these full-grown men in stories amazed me. I had never seen anything like it. Once in a while a tale was told that was worth listening to, but most of them were monotonously uninteresting. They bored me.

5

The A, B, C of Whales

ONE damp morning, with frequent showers falling here and there over the sea and not a drop wetting the brig, Captain Winchester suddenly stopped pacing up and down the weather side of the quarter-deck, threw his head up into the wind, and sniffed the air.

"There's sperm whale about as sure as I live," he said to Mr. Landers. "I smell 'em."

Mr. Landers inhaled the breeze through his nose in jerky little sniffs.

"No doubt about it," he replied. "You could cut the smell with a knife."

I was at the wheel and overheard this talk. I smiled. These old sea dogs, I supposed, were having a little joke. The skipper saw the grin on my face.

"Humph, you don't believe I smell whale, eh?" he said. "I can smell whale like a bird dog smells quail. Take a sniff at the wind. Can't you smell it yourself?"

I gave a few hopeful sniffs. "No," I said, "I can't smell anything unless, perhaps, salt water."

"You've got a poor smeller," returned the captain. "The wind smells rank and oily. That means sperm whale. If I couldn't smell it, I could taste it. I'll give you a plug of tobacco, if we don't raise sperm before dark."

He didn't have to pay the tobacco. Within an hour, we raised a sperm whale spouting far to windward and traveling in the same direction as the brig. The captain hurried to the cabin for his binoculars. As he swung himself into the shrouds to climb to the mast-head, he shouted to me, "Didn't I tell you I could smell 'em?"

The watch was called. The crew of the captain's boat was left to work the ship and Mr. Landers and Gabriel lowered in the larboard and waist boats. Sails were run up and we went skimming away on our first whale hunt. We had a long beat to windward ahead of us and as the whale was moving along at fair speed, remaining below fifteen minutes or so between spouts, it was slow work cutting down the distance that separated us from it.

"See how dat spout slant up in de air?" remarked old Gabriel whom the sight of our first sperm had put in high good humor.

We looked to where the whale was blowing and saw its fountain shoot into the air diagonally, tufted with a cloudy spread of vapor at the top.

"You know why it don't shoot straight up?"

No one knew.

"Dat feller's blow hole in de corner ob his square head—dat's why," said Gabriel. "He blow his fountain out in front of him. Ain't no udder kind o' whale do dat. All de udder kind blow straight up. All de differ in de worl' between dat sperm whale out dere and de bowhead and right whale up nort'. Ain't shaped nothin' a-tall alike. Bowhead and right whale got big curved heads and big curved backs. Sperm whale's about one-third head and his back ain't got no bow to it—not much—jest lies straight out behind his head. He look littler in de water dan de right and bowhead whale. But he ain't. He's as big as de biggest whale dat swims de sea. I've seen a 150 barrel sperm dat measure seventy feet.

"Blow!" added the old Negro as he caught sight of the whale spouting again.

"Bowhead and right whale got no teeth," he continued. "Dey got only long slabs o' baleen hung wit' hair in de upper jaw. Sperm whale got teeth same as you and me—about twenty on a side and all in his lower jaw. Ain't got no teeth in his upper jaw a-tall. His mouth is white inside and his teeth stand up five or six inches out o' his gums and are wide apart and sharp and pointed and look jes' like de teeth of a saw. W'en he open his mouth, his lower jaw fall straight down and his mouth's big enough to take a whale boat inside.

"Sperm whale's fightin' whale. He fight wit' his tail and his teeth. He knock a boat out de water wit' his flukes and he scrunch it into kindlin' wood wit' his teeth. He's got fightin' sense too—he's sly as a fox. W'en I was young feller I was in de sperm trade mysel' and used to ship out o' New Bedford round Cape o' Good Hope for sperm whale ground in Indian Ocean and Sout' Pacific. Once I go on top a sperm whale in a boat an' he turn flukes and lash out wit' his tail but miss us. Den he bring up his old head and take a squint back at us out o' his foxy little eye and begin to slew his body roun' till he get his tail under de boat. But de boat-header too smart fer him and we stern oars and get out o' reach. But de whale didn't know we done backed out o' reach and w'en he bring up dat tail it shoot out o' de water like it was shot out o' a cannon. Mighty fine fer us he miss us dat time.

"But dat don't discourage dat whale a-tall. He swim round and slew round and sight at us out o' his eye and at las' he get under de boat. Den he lift it on de tip o' his tail sky-high and pitch us all in de water. Dat was jes' what he been working for. He swim away and turn round and come shootin' back straight fer dat boat and w'en he get to it, he crush it wit' his teeth and chew it up and shake his head like a mad bulldog until dere warn't nothin' left of dat boat but a lot o' kindlin' wood. But dat warn't all. He swim to a man who wuz lying across an oar to keep afloat and he chew dat man up and spit him out in li'l pieces and we ain't never see nothin' o' dat feller again.

"Guess that whale was goin' to give us all de same medicine, but he ain't have time. De udder boats come up and fill him full o' harpoons and keep stickin' der lances into him and kill him right where he lays and he never had no chance to scoff the rest o' us. But if it ain't fer dem boats, I guess dat feller eat us all jes' like plum duff. Sperm whale, some fighter, believe me.

"Dere he white waters—blow!" added Gabriel as the whale came to the surface again.

"Sperm whale try out de bes' oil," the garrulous old whaleman went on. "Bowhead and right whale got thicker blubber and make more oil, but sperm whale oil de bes'. He got big cistern—what dey call a 'case'—in de top ob his head and it's full o' spermaceti, sloshing about in dere and jes' as clear as water. His old head is always cut off and hoist on deck to bale out dat case. Many times dey find ambergrease (ambergris) floating beside a dead sperm whale. It's solid and yellowish and stuck full o' cuttle feesh beaks dat de whale's done swallowed but ain't digest. Dey makes perfume out o' dat ambergrease and it's worth its weight in gold. I've offen seen it in chunks dat weighed a hundred pounds.

"You see a sperm whale ain't eat nothin' but cuttle feesh—giant squid, dey calls 'em, or devil feesh. Dey certainly is terrible fellers—is dem devil feesh. Got arms twenty or thirty feet long wit' sucking discs all over 'em and a big fat body in de middle ob dese snaky arms, wit' big pop-eyes as big as water buckets and a big black beak like a parrot's to tear its food wit'. Dose devil feesh. Dey certainly is terrible fellers—is dem sperm whale nose 'em out and eat 'em. Some time dey comes to de top and de whale and de cuttle feesh fights it out. I've hearn old whalers say dey seen fights between sperm whale and cuttle feesh but I ain't never seen dat and I reckon mighty few fellers ever did. But when a sperm whale is killed, he spews out chunks o' cuttle feesh and I've seen de water about a dead sperm thick wit' white chunks of cuttle feesh as big as a sea ches' and wit' de suckin' disc still on 'em.

"Blow!" said Gabriel again with his eyes on the whale. "Dat feesh certainly some traveler."

We were hauling closer to the whale. I could see it distinctly by this time and could note how square and black its head was. Its appearance might be compared not inaptly to a box-car glistening in the sun under a fresh coat of black paint. It did not cut the water but pushed it in white foam in front of it.

"Sperm pretty scarce nowadays," Gabriel resumed. "Nothing like as plentiful in Pacific waters as dey used to be in de ole days. Whalers done pretty well thinned 'em out. But long ago, it used to be nothin' to see schools of a hundred, mostly cows wit' three or four big bulls among 'em."

"Any difference between a bowhead and a right whale?" some one asked.

"O good Lord, yes," answered Gabriel. "Big difference. Right whale thinner whale dan a bowhead, ain't got sech thick blubber neither. He's quicker in de water and got nothin' like such long baleen. You ketch right whale in Bering Sea. I ain't never see none in de Arctic Ocean. You ketch bowhead both places. Right whale fightin' feesh, too, but he ain't so dangerous as a sperm."

Let me add that I give this statement of the old whaleman for what it is worth. All books I have ever read on the subject go on the theory that the Greenland or right whale is the same animal as the bowhead. We lowered for a right whale later in the voyage in Bering Sea. To my untrained eyes, it looked like a bowhead which we encountered every few days while on the Arctic Ocean whaling grounds. But there was no doubt or argument about it among the old whalemen aboard. To them it was a "right whale" and nothing else. Old Gabriel may have known what he was talking about. Despite the naturalists, whalers certainly make a pronounced distinction.

By the time Gabriel had imparted all this information, we had worked to within a half mile of our whale which was still steaming along at the rate of knots. They say a sperm whale has ears so small they are scarcely detected, but it has a wonderfully keen sense of hearing for all that. Our whale must have heard us or seen us. At any rate it bade us a sudden goodbye and scurried off unceremoniously over the rim of the world. The boats kept on along the course it was heading for over an hour, but the whale never again favored us with so much as a distant spout. Finally signals from the brig's mast-head summoned us aboard.

As the men had had no practice in the boats before, both boats lowered sail and we started to row back to the vessel. We had pulled about a mile when Mendez, who was acting as boat-steerer, said quietly, "Blow! Blackfish dead ahead."

"Aye, aye," replied Gabriel. "Now stand by, Tomas. I'll jes' lay you aboard one o' dem black-feesh and well teach dese green fellers somethin' 'bout whalin'."

There were about fifty blackfish in the school. They are a species of small toothed whale, from ten to twenty feet long, eight or ten feet in circumference and weighing two or three tons. They were gamboling and tumbling like porpoises. Their black bodies flashed above the surface in undulant curves and I wondered if, when seen at a distance, these little cousins of the sperm had not at some time played their part in establishing the myth of the sea serpent.

"Get ready, Tomas," said Gabriel as we drew near the school.

"Aye, aye, sir," responded Mendez.

Pulling away as hard as we could, we shot among the blackfish. Mendez selected a big one and drove his harpoon into its back. Almost at the same time Mr. Landers's boat became fast to another. Our fish plunged and reared half out of water, rolled and splashed about, finally shot around in a circle and died. Mr. Landers's fish was not fatally hit and when it became apparent it would run away with a tub of line, Little Johnny, the boat-steerer, cut adrift and let it go. Mendez cut our harpoon free and left our fish weltering on the water. Blackfish yield a fairly good quality of oil, but one was too small a catch to potter with. Our adventure among the blackfish was merely practice for the boat crews to prepare them for future encounters with the monarchs of the deep.

6

The Night King

THE crew called Tomas Mendez, the acting third mate, the "Night King." I have forgotten what forecastle poet fastened the name upon him, but it fitted like a glove. In the day watches when the captain and mate were on deck, he was only a quiet, unobtrusive little Negro, insignificant in size and with a bad case of rheumatism. But at night when the other officers were snoring in their bunks below and the destinies of the brig were in his hands, he became an autocrat who ruled with a hand of iron.

He was as black as a bowhead's skin—a lean, scrawny, sinewy little man, stooped about the shoulders and walking with a slight limp. His countenance was imperious. His lips were thin and cruel. His eyes were sharp and sinister. His ebony skin was drawn so tightly over the frame-work of his face that it almost seemed as if it would crack when he smiled. His nose had a domineering Roman curve. He carried his head high. In profile, this little blackamoor suggested the mummied head of some old Pharaoh.

He was a native of the Cape Verde islands. He spoke English with the liquid burr of a Latin. His native tongue was Portuguese. No glimmer of education relieved his mental darkness. It was as though his outside color went all the way through. He could neither read nor write, but he was a good sailor and no better whaleman ever handled a harpoon or laid a boat on a whale's back. For twenty years he had been sailing as boat-steerer on whale ships, and to give the devil his due, he had earned a name for skill and courage in a thousand adventures among sperm, bowhead, and right whales in tropical and frozen seas.

My first impression of the Night King stands out in my memory with cameo distinctness. In the bustle and confusion of setting sails, just after the tug had cut loose from us outside Golden Gate heads, I saw Mendez, like an ebony statue, standing in the waist of the ship, an arm resting easily on the bulwarks, singing out orders in a clear, incisive voice that had in it the ring of steel.

When I shipped, it had not entered my mind that any but white men would be of the ship's company. It was with a shock like a blow in the face that I saw this little colored man singing out orders. I wondered in a dazed sort of way if he was to be in authority over me. I was not long in doubt. When calm had succeeded the first confusion and the crew had been divided into watches, Captain Winchester announced from the break of the poop that "Mr." Mendez would head the port watch. That was my watch. While the captain was speaking, "Mr." Mendez stood like a black Napoleon and surveyed us long and silently. Then suddenly he snapped out a decisive order and the white men jumped to obey. The Night King had assumed his throne.

The Night King and I disliked each other from the start. It may seem petty now that it's all past, but I raged impotently in the bitterness of outraged pride at being ordered about by this black overlord of the quarter-deck. He was not slow to discover my smoldering resentment and came to hate me with a cordiality not far from classic. He kept me busy with some silly job when the other men were smoking their pipes and spinning yarns. If I showed the left-handedness of a landlubber in sailorizing he made me stay on deck my watch below to learn the ropes. If there was dirt or litter to be shoveled overboard, he sang out for me.

"Clean up dat muck dere, you," he would say with fine contempt.

The climax of his petty tyrannies came one night on the run to Honolulu when he charged me with some trifling infraction of ship's rules, of which I was not guilty, and ordered me aloft to sit out the watch on the fore-yard. The yard was broad, the night was warm, the ship was traveling on a steady keel, and physically the punishment was no punishment at all. There was no particular ignominy in the thing, either, for it was merely a joke to the sailors. The sting of it was in having to take such treatment from this small colored person without being able to resent it or help myself.

The very next morning I was awakened by the cry of the lookout on the topsail yard.

"Blow! Blow! There's his old head. Blo-o-o-w! There he ripples. There goes flukes."

Full-lunged and clear, the musical cry came from aloft like a song with little yodeling breaks in the measure. It was the view-halloo of the sea, and it quickened the blood and set the nerves tingling.

"Where away?" shouted the captain, rushing from the cabin with his binoculars.

"Two points on the weather bow, sir," returned the lookout.

For a moment nothing was to be seen but an expanse of yeasty sea. Suddenly into the air shot a fountain of white water—slender, graceful, spreading into a bush of spray at the top. A great sperm was disporting among the white caps.

"Call all hands and clear away the boats," yelled the captain.

Larboard and waist boats were lowered from the davits. Their crews scrambled over the ship's side, the leg-o'-mutton sails were hoisted, and the boats, bending over as the wind caught them, sped away on the chase. The Night King went as boat-steerer of the waist boat. I saw him smiling to himself as he shook the kinks out of his tub-line and laid his harpoons in position in the bows—harpoons with no bomb-guns attached to the spear-shanks.

In the distance, a slow succession of fountains gleamed in the brilliant tropical sunshine like crystal lamps held aloft on fairy pillars. Suddenly the tell-tale beacons of spray went out. The whale had sounded. Over the sea, the boats quartered like baffled foxhounds to pick up the lost trail.

Between the ship and the boats, the whale came quietly to the surface at last and lay perfectly still, taking its ease, sunning itself and spouting lazily. The captain, perched in the ship's cross-trees, signaled its position with flags, using a code familiar to whalemen. The Night King caught the message first. He turned quickly to the boatheader at the tiller and pointed. Instantly the boat came about, the sailors shifted from one gunwale to the other, the big sail swung squarely out and filled. All hands settled themselves for the run to close quarters.

With thrilling interest, I watched the hunt from the ship's forward bulwarks, where I stood grasping a shroud to prevent pitching overboard. Down a long slant of wind, the boat ran free with the speed of a greyhound, a white plume of spray standing high on either bow. The Night King stood alert and cool, one foot on the bow seat, balancing a harpoon in his hands. The white background of the bellying sail threw his tense figure into relief. Swiftly, silently, the boat stole upon its quarry until but one long sea lay between. It rose upon the crest of the wave and poised there for an instant like some great white-winged bird of prey. Then sweeping down the green slope, it struck the whale bows-on and beached its keel out of the water on its glistening hack. As it struck, the Night King let fly one harpoon and another, driving them home up to the wooden hafts with all the strength of his lithe arms.

The sharp bite of the iron in its vitals stirred the titanic mass of flesh and blood from perfect stillness into a frenzy of sudden movement that churned the water of the sea into white froth. The great head went under, the giant back curved down like the whirling surface of some mighty fly-wheel, the vast flukes, like some black demon's arm, shot into the air. Left and right and left again, the great tail thrashed, smiting the sea with thwacks which could have been heard for miles. It struck the boat glancingly with its bare tip, yet the blow stove a great hole in the bottom timbers, lifted the wreck high in air, and sent the sailors sprawling into the sea. Then the whale sped away with the speed of a limited express. It had not been vitally wounded. Over the distant horizon, it passed out of sight, blowing up against the sky fountains of clear water unmixed with blood.

The other boat hurried to the rescue and the crew gathered up the half-drowned sailors perched on the bottom of the upturned boat or clinging to floating sweeps. Fouled in the rigging of the sail, held suspended beneath the wreck in the green crystal of the sea water, they found the Night King, dead.

When the whale crushed the boat—at the very moment, it must have been—the Night King had snatched the knife kept fastened in a sheath on the bow thwart and with one stroke of the razor blade, severed the harpoon lines. He thus released the whale and prevented it from dragging the boat away in its mad race. The Night King's last act had saved the lives of his companions.

I helped lift the body over the rail. We laid it on the quarter-deck near the skylight. It lurched and shifted in a ghastly sort of way as the ship rolled, the glazed eyes open to the blue sky. The captain's Newfoundland dog came and sniffed at the corpse.

Sheltered from the captain's eye behind the galley, the Kanaka cabin boy shook a furtive fist at the dead man and ground out between clenched teeth, "You black devil, you'll never kick me again."

Standing not ten feet away, the mate cracked a joke to the second mate and the two laughed uproariously. The work of the ship went on all around.

Looking upon the dead thing lying there, I thought of the pride with which the living man had borne himself in the days of his power. I beheld in fancy the silent, lonely, imperious little figure, pacing to and fro on the weather side of the quarter-deck—to and fro under the stars. I saw him stop in the darkness by the wheel, as his custom was, to peer down into the lighted binnacle and say in vibrant tones, "Keep her steady," or "Let her luff." I saw him buttoned up in his overcoat to keep the dew of the tropical night from his rheumatic joints, slip down the poop ladder and stump forward past the try-works to see how things fared in the bow.

Again I heard his nightly cry to the lookout on the forecastle head, "Keep a bright lookout dere, you," and saw him limp back to continue his vigil, pacing up and down. The qualities that had made him hated when he was indeed the Night King flooded back upon me, but I did not forget the courage of my enemy that had redeemed them all and made him a hero in the hour of death.

In the afternoon, old Nelson sat on the deck beside the corpse and with palm and needle fashioned a long canvas bag. Into this the dead man was sewed with a weight of brick and sand at his feet.

At sunset, when all hands were on deck for the dog watch, they carried the body down on the main deck and with feet to the sea, laid it on the gang-plank which had been removed from the rail. There in the waist the ship's company gathered with uncovered heads. Over all was the light of the sunset, flushing the solemn, rough faces and reddening the running white-caps of the sea. The captain called me to him and placed a Bible in my hands.

"Read a passage of scripture," he said.

Dumbfounded that I should be called upon to officiate at the burial service over the man I had hated, I took my stand on the main hatch at the head of the body and prepared to obey orders. No passage to fit my singular situation occurred to me and I opened the book at random. The leaves fell apart at the seventh chapter of Matthew and I read aloud the section beginning:

"Judge not, that ye be not judged. For with what judgment ye judge, ye shall be judged; and with what measure ye mete, it shall be measured to you again."

At the close of the reading the captain called for "The Sweet Bye and Bye" and the crew sang the verses of the old hymn solemnly. When the full-toned music ceased, two sailors tilted the gang-plank upwards and the remains of the Night King slid off and plunged into the ocean.

As the body slipped toward the water, a Kanaka sailor caught up a bucket of slop which he had set aside for the purpose, and dashed its filth over the corpse from head to foot. Wide-eyed with astonishment, I looked to see instant punishment visited upon this South Sea heathen who so flagrantly violated the sanctities of the dead. But not a hand was raised, not a word of disapproval was uttered. The Kanaka had but followed a whaler's ancient custom. The parting insult to the dead was meant to discourage the ghost from ever coming back to haunt the brig.

7

Dreams of Liberty

A T midnight after the burial, we raised the volcanic fire of Mauna Loa dead ahead. Sailors declare that a gale always follows a death at sea and the wind that night blew hard. But we cracked on sail and next morning we were gliding in smooth water along the shore of the island of Hawaii with the great burning mountain towering directly over us and the smoke from the crater swirling down through our rigging.

We loafed away three pleasant weeks among the islands, loitering along the beautiful sea channels, merely killing time until Captain Shorey should arrive from San Francisco by steamer. Once we sailed within distant view of Molokai. It was as beautiful in its tropical verdure as any of the other islands of the group, but its very name was fraught with sinister and tragic suggestiveness—it was the home of the lepers, the island of the Living Death.

We did not anchor at any time. None of the whaling fleet which meets here every spring ever anchors. The lure of the tropical shores is strong and there would be many desertions if the ships lay in port. We sailed close to shore in the day time, often entering Honolulu harbor, but at night we lay off and on, as the sailor term is—that is we tacked off shore and back again, rarely venturing closer than two or three miles, a distance the hardiest swimmer, bent upon desertion, would not be apt to attempt in those shark-haunted waters.

Many attempts to escape from vessels of the whaling fleet occur in the islands every year. We heard many yarns of these adventures. A week before we arrived, five sailors had overpowered the night watch aboard their ship and escaped to shore in a whale boat. They were captured in the hills back of Honolulu and returned to their vessel. This is usually the fate of runaways. A standing reward of $25 a man is offered by whaling ships for the capture and return of deserters, consequently all the natives of the islands, especially the police, are constantly on the lookout for runaways from whaling crews.

When we drew near the islands the runaway fever became epidemic in the forecastle. Each sailor had his own little scheme for getting away. Big Taylor talked of knocking the officers of the night watch over the head with a belaying-pin and stealing ashore in a boat. Ole Oleson cut up his suit of oil-skins and sewed them into two air-tight bags with one of which under each arm, he proposed to float ashore. Bill White, an Englishman, got possession of a lot of canvas from the cabin and was clandestinely busy for days making it into a boat in which he fondly hoped to paddle ashore some fine night in the dark of the moon. "Slim," our Irish grenadier, stuffed half his belongings into his long sea-boots which he planned to press into service both as carry-alls and life-preservers. Peter Swenson, the forecastle's baby boy, plugged up some big empty oil cans and made life buoys of them by fastening a number of them together.

Just at the time when the forecastle conspiracies were at their height we killed a thirteen-foot shark off Diamond Head. Our catch was one of a school of thirty or forty monsters that came swarming about the brig, gliding slowly like gray ghosts only a few feet below the surface, nosing close to the ship's side for garbage and turning slightly on their sides to look out of their evil eyes at the sailors peering down upon them over the rail.

Long John, the boat-steerer, got out a harpoon, and standing on the bulwarks shot the iron up to the wooden haft into the back of one of the sharks, the spear-point of the weapon passing through the creature and sticking out on the under side. The stout manila hemp attached to the harpoon had been made fast to the fore-bitt. It was well that this was so, for the shark plunged and fought with terrific fury, lashing the sea into white froth. But the harpoon had pierced a vital part and in a little while the great fish ceased its struggles and lay still, belly up on the surface.

It was hauled close alongside, and a boat having been lowered, a large patch of the shark's skin was cut off. Then the carcass was cut adrift. The skin was as rough as sandpaper. It was cut into small squares, which were used in scouring metal and for all the polishing purposes for which sandpaper serves ashore.

Life aboard the brig seemed less intolerable thereafter, and an essay at escape through waters infested by such great, silent, ravenous sea-wolves seemed a hazard less desirable than before. Taylor talked no more about slugging the night watch. Slim unpacked his sea-boots and put his effects back into his chest. Peter threw his plugged oil cans overboard. Bill White turned his canvas boat into curtains for his bunk, and Ole Oleson voiced in the lilting measure of Scandinavia his deep regret that he had cut up a valuable suit of oil-skins.

The captain of one of the whaling ships came one afternoon to visit our skipper and his small boat was left dragging in our wake as the brig skimmed along under short sail. It occurred to me, and at the same time to my two Kanaka shipmates, that here was a fine opportunity to escape. It was coming on dusk, and if we could get into the boat and cut loose we might have a splendid chance to get away. The Kanakas and I climbed over the bow, intending to let ourselves into the sea and drift astern to the boat, but the breeze had freshened and the brig was traveling so fast we did not believe we could catch the boat; and if we failed to do so, we might confidently expect the sharks to finish us. We abandoned the plan after we had remained squatting on the stays over the bow for a half hour considering our chances and getting soaked to the skin from the dashing spray.

A pathetic incident grew out of the visit of the captain from the other ship. Tomas Mendez's brother, a boat-steerer, came aboard with the boat's crew. He was a young Negro whom all the boat-steerers and officers knew. He came swinging lightly over our rail, laughing and happy over the prospect of seeing his brother.

"Hello, fellers," he called to the Portuguese officers and boat-steerers who welcomed him.

"Where's my brooder?"

"Dead, my boy," said one of the boat-steerers gently.

"Dead?" echoed Mendez.

He staggered back. When he had heard the details of his brother's death, he burst into tears. All the time his skipper remained aboard, the poor fellow stood by the cooper's bench and sobbed.

While drifting at the mouth of Honolulu harbor one morning, Captain Winchester called for a boat's crew to row him ashore. All hands wanted to go. I was one of the lucky ones to be chosen. The morning was calm and beautiful, the water was smooth, and we pulled away with a will.

The city looked inviting at the foot of its green mountains, its quaint houses embowered in tropical foliage. On our starboard beam rose the fine, bold promontory of Diamond Head, and in between the headland and the city lay Waikiki, the fashionable bathing beach.

We could see the bathers taking the surf in the bright morning sunlight, while beyond stretched a delectable wooded country, above the tops of whose trees peeped manors and villas of wealthy citizens.

We reached the long pier at last and tied up the boat. While the captain went into the city the sailors remained on the dock in charge of Long John, the boat-steerer. Three snaky-eyed Kanaka policemen in blue uniforms hung about, watching our every movement. We were not allowed to stir off the dock. There was a street corner within a stone's throw. A little red brick store stood upon it. A lazy Kanaka lounged against the building, smoking a cigarette. That corner fascinated me. If I only could dodge around it! How near it seemed, and yet how unattainable!

But if we sailormen could not get into town, we at least had the freedom of the long pier. This was several hundred feet long and piled thick with freight of all descriptions, which shut its harbor end from view. With a casual and indifferent air I sauntered out along the pier. In a moment I was hidden behind the merchandise from the unsuspecting Long John and the policemen. I soon reached the harbor end. I saw that a sharp curve in the shore line brought the part of the pier on which I was standing close to land. It seemed easy to dive off the pier, swim past a big four-masted English ship unloading alongside, gain the land, and escape to the cane fields which swept up to the edge of the city.

I sat down behind some freight and began to take off my shoes. I had one off when a barefooted Kanaka suddenly stepped into view from behind a pile of bales and boxes. He was tiptoeing and peering about him furtively. I knew him for a spy instantly. Directly he saw me staring at him he looked as guilty as one taken in crime, and slunk away sheepishly. I knew he was on his way to inform on me and made up my mind not to get my clothes wet by any hopeless attempt to run away.

I put my shoe back on and strolled back toward the boat. I saw one of my shipmates—it was Richard, the deep-water German sailor—walking up the gangplank of the English ship alongside the dock. I followed him. When we reached the deck, we saw a gang of sailors working about an open hatch.

"Hello, mates," said Richard. "We are merchant seamen and want to clear out from a blooming whaler. Stow us away, won't you?"

The sailors didn't seem to take kindly to the proposition. Perhaps they were afraid of getting into trouble. But they told us we might go down in the fore-peak of the ship and stow ourselves away. Richard and I climbed down three decks and found ourselves in the chain lockers deep in the ship's bow. It was pitch dark down there and we lay upon the ship's cable in the farthest corners. For three hours we huddled there in silence.

Just when we were beginning to congratulate ourselves that our escape would be successful, the hatch was pulled off suddenly and three Kanaka policemen with drawn clubs came leaping down upon us.

"Come out of this, you," they yelled, swearing at us and brandishing their billets. The jig was up; resistance would have got us only broken heads.

We were led upon deck and escorted toward the gangway for the pier. But I was for one more try before giving up. Suddenly I darted for the rail on the harbor side of the ship. We were in the waist and the bulwarks reached about to my breast. Before the Kanaka policemen had recovered from their surprise I had plunged head first over the rail and dived into the water twenty or thirty feet below. When I came to the surface I struck out for shore with all my might. It was only a short swim. I soon made the land and dragged myself, dripping brine, out upon a beach.

I glanced toward the pier. The policemen, with a crowd at their backs, were dashing for me along shore. I started for the cane fields, but in my wet and heavy clothes I stumbled along as if there was lead in my shoes. Perhaps I ran a quarter of a mile. My pursuers gained on me steadily. I was drawing near a cane field, in which I felt I should be able to lose myself; but before reaching it, my pursuers sprang upon me and bore me to the ground. Then, with a policeman on either side of me, I was marched back to the brig's boat.

The populace had turned out royally in my honor and I passed through a lane of brown humanity that bent round eyes upon me and chortled and spluttered Kanaka and seemed to get a huge amount of enjoyment out of my capture. As my captors paraded me onto the pier, who should be there waiting for me but Captain Shorey, our new skipper, just arrived from San Francisco by steamer. He stood with feet wide apart and arms folded on his breast and looked at me steadily with stern, cold eyes. In my wet clothes I cut a sorry figure. I felt ashamed of myself and realized that this introduction to my new captain was not all it should have been. Captain Winchester had nothing to say to Richard and me on the long pull back to the brig. Once aboard, he drew a pint of Jamaica rum from his pocket and gave every man of the boat's crew, except us, a swig. But no penalty of any sort was imposed upon us for our escapade. This surprised us.

8

Gabriel's Little Drama

ON a bright, sunshiny morning a few days later, with a light breeze just ruffling the harbor, the brig with her sails laid back and her head pointed seaward was drifting with the ebb tide perhaps a mile and a quarter off shore between Honolulu and Diamond Head. Captain Winchester had set out for the city in a whale boat. Those of the sailors left aboard were idling forward. Mr. Landers, the mate, sat by the skylight on the poop, reading a magazine. Second mate Gabriel and the cooper were busy at the cooper's bench in the waist. No one else was on deck and I resolved to attempt again to escape. The situation seemed made to order.

In the warm weather of the tropics, I had often seen old man Landers, when there was nothing doing on deck, sit and read by the hour without ever looking up. I hoped that this morning his magazine would prove of absorbing interest. Gabriel and the cooper were intent upon their work. As for the sailors, I told them I was going to try to swim ashore and if I were discovered and they had to lower for me, I asked them to hurry as little as possible so I might have every chance to get away.

For my adventure I wore a blue flannel shirt, dungaree trousers, and my blue cap. I tied my shoes together with a rope yarn, which I slipped baldric-fashion over my shoulder. In the belt at my waist I carried a sailor's sheath knife. With this I had a foolish idea that I might defend myself against sharks. Without attracting attention, I slipped over the bow, climbed down by the bob-stays, and let myself into the sea. I let myself wash silently astern past the ship's side and struck out for shore, swimming on my side without splash or noise, and looking back to watch developments aboard.

I am convinced to this day that if I had not been in the water, old Landers would have kept his nose in that magazine for an hour or so and drowsed and nodded over it as I had seen him do dozens of times before. Either my good angel, fearful of the sharks, or my evil genius, malignantly bent upon thwarting me, must have poked the old fellow in the ribs. At any rate, he rose from his chair and stepped to the taff-rail with a pair of binoculars in his hand. He placed the glasses to his eyes and squinted toward the pier to see whether or not the captain had reached shore. I don't know whether he saw the captain or not, but he saw me.

"Who's that overboard?" he shouted.

I did not answer. Then he recognized me.

"Hey, you," he cried, calling me by name, "come back here."

I kept on swimming.

"Lay aft here, a boat's crew," Mr. Landers sang out.

Gabriel and the cooper ran to the quarter-deck and stared at me. The sailors came lounging aft along the rail. Mr. Landers and Gabriel threw the boat's falls from the davit posts. The sailors strung out across the deck to lower the boat.

"Lower away," shouted Mr. Landers.

One end of the boat went down rapidly. The other end jerked and lurched and seemed to remain almost stationary. I wondered whether my shipmates were bungling purposely. Mr. Landers and Gabriel sprang among them, brushed them aside and lowered the boat themselves. A crew climbed down the brig's side into the boat. Old Gabriel went as boatheader. In a jiffy the sweeps were shot into place, the boat was shoved off, and the chase was on.

All this had taken time. As the ship was drifting one way and I was quartering off in an almost opposite direction, I must have been nearly a half mile from the vessel when Gabriel started to run me down.

I swam on my side with a long, strong stroke that fast swimmers used to fancy before the Australian crawl came into racing vogue. I was swimming as I never in my life swam before—swimming for liberty. All my hope and heart, as well as all my strength, lay in every stroke. The clear, warm salt water creamed about my head and sometimes over it. I was making time. Swimming on my side, I could see everything that was happening behind me. As the boat came after me I noticed there was but a slight ripple of white water about the prow. Plainly it was not making great speed.

"Pull away, my boys. We ketch dat feller," sang out Gabriel.

Wilson at the midship oar "caught a crab" and tumbled over backwards, his feet kicking in the air. Wilson was a good oarsman. He was my friend. A hundred yards more and Walker at the tub oar did the same. He also was my friend.

The boys were doing their best to help me—to give me a chance. I knew it. Gabriel knew it, too. The crafty old Negro recognized the crisis. I could not hear what he said or see all that he did, but the boys told me about it afterwards. It must have been a pretty bit of acting.

Suddenly Gabriel half rose from his seat and peered anxiously ahead.

"My God!" he cried, "dat poor feller, he drown. Pull, my boys. Oh, good God!"

The sailors at the sweeps had their backs to me. It was a good long swim and the water was full of sharks. It was not difficult to make them believe that I was verging on tragedy.

"Dere he go down!" Gabriel's voice was broken and sobbing. "He t'row his hands up. He underneath de water. I cain't see him. Oh, dat poor feller! No, dere he come up again—oh, good Lord! Pull away, my bully boys, pull away. We save him yet."

Surely the stage lost a star when Gabriel became a whaler. The old Thespian was good—he was great. His acting carried conviction. The sailors believed I was drowning. They leaned upon their oars with a will. The sweeps bent beneath the powerful strokes. The boat jumped through the water. I noted the increased speed by the white spray that began to stand at the bow. Gabriel helped along the speed by forward lurches of his body, pushing at the same time upon the stroke oar. All the while he kept shouting:

"We save him yet, dat poor feller! Pull away, my boys."

The boat came up rapidly. In a little while it was almost upon me. I tried to dodge it by darting off at right angles. It was no use— Gabriel slewed his tiller and the boat came swishing round upon me, I had played the game out to the last and I was beaten—that was all. I caught the gunwale near the bow and pulled myself into the boat.

"You make dam good swim, my boy," said old Gabriel, smiling at me as he brought the boat around and headed back for the ship.

I had made a good swim. I was fully a mile from the brig. I was not much over a half mile from shore. I looked across the sunlit, dancing blue water to the land. How easy it would have been to swim it! How easy it would have been after I had crawled out upon the sands to hide in the nearby mountains and live on wild fruit until the ship started for the north and all danger of capture was past.

No land could have seemed more beautiful. Groves of banana, orange, and cocoanut trees held out their fruit to me. Forests swept to the summits of the mountains. Flowers were in riotous bloom everywhere. I could almost count the ribs in the glossy fronds of the palms. I could hear the soft crash of the combers on the coral beaches of those enchanted shores. It all looked like paradise and I had missed it by half a mile.

When I reached the brig, Mr. Landers permitted me to put on dry clothing and then put me in irons, as the sea phrase is. This consisted in fastening my hands together in front of me with a pair of steel handcuffs of the ordinary kind used by sheriffs and policemen everywhere. Then he made me sit on the main hatch until Captain Winchester came back from Honolulu, along toward sundown.

"What's the matter with that man?" roared the captain as he swung over the rail and his eyes lighted on me.

"He jumped overboard and tried to swim ashore," said Mr. Landers in his nasal Cape Cod drawl.

"Why didn't you get my rifle and shoot him?" thundered the captain.

"Well," returned Mr. Landers, "I don't shoot folks."

After supper the captain stuck his head out of the cabin gangway.

"Come down here, you," he said. I stepped into the cabin, now bright with lighted lamps. The captain glared at me savagely.

"You want to give me a bad name with Captain Shorey when he takes command, do you?" he shouted. "You want to make it appear I have been hard on my men, eh? You think you're a smart sea lawyer, but I'll teach you the bitterest lesson you ever learned. We are bound for the Arctic Ocean. There are no ships up there but whale ships, and we do as we please. I have been sailing to the Arctic for thirteen years as master and mate of whale ships and I know just how far I can go in dealing with a man without making myself liable to law. I am going to make it as rough for you as I know how to make it. I will put you over the jumps right. I will punish you to the limit. This ship is going to be a floating hell for you for the rest of the voyage. And when we get back to San Francisco you can prosecute me all you please."

He drew a key from his pocket and unlocked one manacle. It dropped from one wrist and dangled from the other.

"Boy," he said to the Kanaka cabin boy, who has been listening with open mouth and bulging eyes to this tirade, "get this man a cup of water and a biscuit."

I had had nothing to eat since breakfast, and I sat down at the cabin table and ate my one hardtack and drank my quart tin of water with a relish. After my meal, the captain fastened my handcuff again and jerked a little hatch out of the floor.

"Get down there," he said.

I climbed down and he clapped the hatch on again. I was in darkness except for the light that filtered from the cabin lamps through the four cracks of the hatch. When my eyes had become accustomed to the dimness, I made out that I was in the ship's run, where the provisions for the captain's table were stored. I rummaged about as well as I could in my handcuffs and found a sack of raisins open and a box of soda crackers. To these I helped myself generously. From a forecastle viewpoint they were rare dainties, and I filled my empty stomach with them. I had not tasted anything so good since I had my last piece of pie ashore.

Pie! Dear me! One doesn't know how good it is—just common pie baked in a bakery and sold at the corner grocery—until one cannot get it and has had nothing but salt horse and cracker hash for months. I used to yearn for pie by day and dream of pie by night.

At bedtime the captain snatched the hatch off again and tossed me down my blankets. I bundled up in them as best I could and slept with my manacles on.

I was kept in irons on bread and water for five days and nights. Sometimes in the daytime, with one handcuff unlocked and hanging from my other wrist, I was put at slushing down the main boom or washing paint-work. But for the most part I was held a close prisoner in the run, being called to the cabin table three times a day for my bread and water. Finally, when Captain Shorey came aboard and assumed command and the vessel headed for the north, I was released and sent to the forecastle. My shipmates proved Job's comforters and were filled with gloomy predictions regarding my future.

"I pity you from now on," each one said.

But their prophecies proved false. After Captain Shorey took charge of the ship Mr. Winchester became mate. As mate he was, as may be said, the ship's foreman, directing the work of the men, and was in much more intimate contact with the sailors than when he had been skipper. In his new capacity he had much greater opportunity to make it unpleasant for me in a thousand ways. But for some reason or other he never made good that ferocious speech he had delivered to me in the cabin.

When other green hands bungled, he damned them in round terms for their awkwardness. When I blundered he showed me how to correct my error. "Not that way, my boy," he would say. "Do it this way."

When I took my trick at the wheel he would often spin a yarn or crack a joke with me. He loaned me books from time to time. In the Bering Sea, when he got out his rifle and shot okchug seals as they lay basking on cakes of ice, he almost invariably took me with him in the boat to bring back the kill. In short, he treated me more considerately than he treated any other man in the forecastle and before the voyage was over we had become fast friends.

9

Through the Roaring Forties

BEFORE leaving the islands, we shipped a Portuguese Negro boat-steerer to take the place of the Night King. He was coal-black, had a wild roll to his eyes, an explosive, spluttering way of talking, looked strikingly like a great ape, and had little more than simian intelligence. His feet had the reputation of being the largest feet in the Hawaiian Islands. When I had seen them I was prepared to believe they were the largest in the world. He was dubbed "Big Foot" Louis, and the nickname stuck to him during the voyage. He came aboard barefooted. I don't know whether he could find any shoes in the islands big enough to fit him or not. Anyway, he didn't need shoes in the tropics.

When we began to get north into cold weather he needed them badly, and there were none on board large enough for him to get his toes in. The captain went through his stock of Eskimo boots, made of walrus hide and very elastic, but they were too small. When we entered the region of snow, Louis was still running about the deck barefooted. As a last resort he sewed himself a pair of canvas shoes—regular meal sacks—and wore them through snow and blizzard and during the cold season when we were in the grip of the Bering Sea ice pack. Up around Bering Straits the captain hired an Eskimo to make a pair of walrus hide boots big enough for Louis to wear, and Louis wore them until we got back to San Francisco and went ashore in them. I met him wandering along Pacific Street in his walrus hides. However, he soon found a pair of brogans which he could wear with more or less comfort.

One night while I was knocking about the Barbary Coast with my shipmates we heard dance music and the sound of revelry coming from behind the swinging doors of the Bow Bells saloon, a free-and-easy resort. We stepped inside. Waltzing around the room with the grace of a young bowhead out of water was "Big Foot" Louis, his arm around the waist of a buxom Negress, and on his feet nothing but a pair of red socks. We wondered what had become of his shoes and spied them on the piano, which the "professor" was vigorously strumming. Louis seemed to be having more fun than anybody, and was perfectly oblivious to the titters of the crowd and to the fact that it was not *de rigueur* on the Barbary Coast to dance in one's socks.

We left the Hawaiian Islands late in March and, standing straight north, soon left the tropics behind, never to see them again on the voyage. As we plunged into the "roaring forties" we struck our first violent storm. The fury of the gale compelled us to heave to under staysails and drift, lying in the troughs of the seas and riding the waves sidewise. The storm was to me a revelation of what an ocean gale could be. Old sailors declared they never had seen anything worse. The wind shrieked and whistled in the rigging like a banshee. It was impossible to hear ordinary talk and the men had to yell into each other's ears. We put out oil bags along the weather side to keep the waves from breaking. But despite the oil that spread from them over the water, giant seas frequently broke over the brig. One crushed the waist boat into kindling wood and sent its fragments flying all over the deck. We were fortunate to have several other extra boats in the hold against just such an emergency. Waves sometimes filled the ship to the top of the bulwarks and the sailors waded about up to their breasts in brine until the roll of the vessel spilled the water overboard or it ran back into the sea through the scuppers and hawse-holes.

The waves ran as high as the topsail yard. They would pile up to windward of us, gaining height and volume until we had to look up almost vertically to see the tops. Just as a giant comber seemed ready to break in roaring foam and curl over and engulf us, the staunch little brig would slip up the slope of water and ride over the summit in safety. Then the sea would shoot out on the other side of the vessel with a deafening hiss like that of a thousand serpents and rush skyward again, the wall of water streaked and shot with foam and looking like a polished mass of jade or agate.

I had not imagined water could assume such wild and appalling shapes. Those monster waves seemed replete with malignant life, roaring out their hatred of us and watching alertly with their devilish foam-eyes for a chance to leap upon us and crush us or sweep us to death on their crests.

I became genuinely seasick now for the first time. A little touch of seasickness I had experienced in the tropics was as nothing. To the rail

I went time and again to give up everything within me, except my immortal soul, to the mad gods of sea. For two days I lay in my bunk. I tried pickles, fat bacon, everything that any sailor recommended, all to no purpose. I would have given all I possessed for one fleeting moment upon something level and still, something that did not plunge and lurch and roll from side to side and rise and fall. I think the most wretched part of seasickness is the knowledge that you cannot run away from it, that you are penned in with it, that go where you will, on the royal yard or in the bilge, you cannot escape the ghastly nightmare even for a minute.

There is no use fighting it and no use dosing yourself with medicines or pickles or lemons or fat meat. Nothing can cure it. In spite of everything it will stay with you until it has worked its will to the uttermost, and then it will go away at last of its own accord, leaving you a wan, limp wreck.

I may add, to correct a general impression, that it is impossible to become seasoned to seasickness. One attack does not render the victim immune from future recurrences. I was very sick once again on the voyage. After a season ashore, the best sailors are liable to seasickness, especially if they encounter rough weather soon after leaving port. Some time later we were frozen solidly in Bering Sea for three weeks. When a storm swell from the south broke up the ice and the motionless brig began suddenly to rock and toss on a heavy sea, every mother's son aboard, including men who had been to sea all their lives, was sick. Not one escaped.

During the storm we kept a man at the wheel and another on the try-works as a lookout. One day during my trick at the wheel, I was probably responsible for a serious accident, though it might have happened with the most experienced sailor at the helm. To keep the brig in the trough of the seas, I was holding her on a certain point of the compass, but the big waves buffeted the vessel about with such violence that my task was difficult. Captain Shorey was standing within arm's length of me, watching the compass. A sea shoved the brig's head to starboard and, as if it had been lying in ambush for just such an opportunity, a giant comber came curling in high over the stern. It smashed me into the wheel and for an instant I was buried under twenty feet of crystal water that made a green twilight all about us.

Then the wave crashed down ponderously upon the deck and I was standing in clear air again. To my astonishment, the captain was no longer beside me. I thought he had been washed overboard. The wave had lifted him upon its top, swept him high over the skylight the entire length of the quarter-deck and dropped him on the main deck in the waist. His right leg was broken below the knee. Sailors and boat-steerers rushed to him and carried him into the cabin, where Mr. Winchester set the broken bones. We put into Unalaska a week later and the surgeon of the revenue cutter *Bear* reset the leg. This was in the last days of March. The captain was on crutches in July, when we caught our first whale.

The storm did not blow itself out. It blew us out of it. We must have drifted sidewise with the seas about six hundred miles. At dawn of the second day, after leaving the fury of the forties behind, we were bowling along in smooth water with all sails set. The sky was clear and the sea like hammered silver. Far ahead a mountain rose into the sky—a wedge-shaped peak, silver-white with snow, its foot swathed in purple haze. It rose above Unimak Pass, which connects the Pacific Ocean and Bering Sea between Unimak and Ugamok islands of the Fox Island chain.

Unimak Pass is ten miles broad, and its towering shores are sheer, black, naked rock. Mr. Winchester, who had assumed command after the captain had broken his leg, set a course to take us directly through the passage. Running before a light breeze that bellied all our sails, we began to draw near the sea gorge at the base of the mountain. Then, without warning, from over the horizon came a savage white squall, blotting out mountain, pass, sea, and sky.

I never saw bad weather blow up so quickly. One moment the ship was gliding over a smooth sea in bright sunlight. The next, a cloud as white and almost as thick as wool had closed down upon it; snow was falling heavily in big, moist flakes, a stiff wind was heeling the vessel on its side, and we could not see ten feet beyond the tip of the jib boom.

The wind quickened into a gale. By fast work we managed to furl sails and double-reef the topsail before they carried away. Soon the deck was white with four or five inches of snow. On the forecastle head Big Foot Louis was posted as lookout. Everybody was anxious. Mr. Winchester took his stand close by the main shrouds at the break of the poop and kept gazing ahead through his glasses into the mist. The sailors and boat-steerers crowded the forward rails, peering vainly into the swirling fog. Big Foot Louis bent forward with his hand shielding his eyes from the falling snow.

"Land, land!" he cried.

If it were land that Louis saw through the clouds and blinding snow, it was mighty close. Our doom seemed sealed. We expected the ship to crash bows-on upon the rocks. We nerved ourselves for the shock. A momentary vision of shipwreck on those bleak coasts in snow and storm obsessed me. But Louis's eyes had deceived him. The ship went riding on its stately way through the blinding snow before the gale.

The situation was ticklish, if not critical. We had been headed squarely for the passage before the storm closed down. Now we could not see where we were going. If we held directly upon our course we were safe. If the gale blew us even slightly out of our way, shipwreck and death on the rock-bound shore awaited us. Which would it be?

Mr. Winchester was a man of iron nerve. He demonstrated this now as he did many times afterward. He was as skillful a navigator as he was a fearless one. He knew his reckonings were good. He knew that when the squall shut out the world the brig's nose was pointed directly at the center of Unimak Pass. So he did not veer to east or west, or seek to tack back from the dangerous coasts on our bows, but drove the vessel straight upon its course into the blank white wall of mist and snow.

An hour later the squall lifted as quickly as it had come. Blue skies and sunshine came back. We found ourselves almost becalmed on a placid sea. To the south lay the outline of a lofty coast.

A boat-steerer bustled forward. "We are in Bering Sea," he said with a laugh.

We had shot through the narrow channel without sighting the shores. I have often wondered just how close to port or starboard death was to us that morning on the black cliffs of Unimak Pass.

10

In the Ice

FROM Unalaska, into which port we put to have the captain's leg attended to, the brig stood northwesterly for the spring whaling on the bowhead and right whale grounds off the Siberian coast. We were a week's sail from the Fox Islands when we encountered our first ice. It appeared in small chunks floating down from the north. The blocks became more numerous until they dappled the sea. They grew in size. Strings and floes appeared. Then we brought up against a great ice field stretching to the north as far as the eye could see. It was all floe ice broken into hummocks and pressure ridges and pinnacles, with level spaces between. There were no towering bergs such as are launched into the sea from the glaciers on the Greenland coast and the Pacific coast of Alaska. The highest berg

I saw on the voyage was not more than forty feet high. It was composed of floe ice which had been forced upward by the pressure of the pack.

The crow's nest was now rigged and placed in position on the cross-trees abaft the foremast, between the topsail and the fore-top-gallant-sail yard. It was a square box of heavy white canvas nailed upon a wooden framework. When a man stood in it the canvas sides reached to his breast and were a protection against the bitter winds. From early morning until dark an officer and a boat-steerer occupied the crow's nest and kept a constant lookout for whales.

As soon as we struck the ice the captain's slop-chest was broken open and skin clothes were dealt out to the men. Accoutred for cold weather, I wore woolen underwear and yarn socks next my flesh; an outer shirt of squirrel skin with hood or parka; pants and vest of hair seal of the color and sheen of newly minted silver; a coat of dogskin that reached almost to my knees; a dogskin cap; deerskin socks with the hair inside over my yarn socks; walrus-hide boots and walrus-hide mittens over yarn mittens. The walrus-boots were fastened by a gathering string just below the knees and by thongs of tanned skin about the ankle. Some of the men wore heavy reindeer-skin coats.

The skin clothes worn by the officers and boat-steerers were of finer quality and more pretentious. Perhaps the handsomest costume was that of Little Johnny. It consisted of coat, vest, and trousers of silvery hair-seal, with the edges of the coat trimmed with the snow white fur of fur-seal pups. With this he wore a black dogskin cap and walrus-hide boots.

While we were among the ice, the officer in the crow's nest directed the course of the brig. Whaling officers are great fellows to show their skill by just grazing dangerous ice. Many a time we green hands stood with our hearts in our mouths as the ship seemed about to crash into a berg bows-on.

"Starboard, sir," the helmsman would respond.

"Starboard," would come the order from aloft.

The bow would swing slowly to one side and the berg would go glancing along the rail so close perhaps that we could have grabbed a snowball off some projection.

"Steady," the officer would call.

"Steady, sir." The bow would stop in its lateral swing.

"Port."

"Port, sir". The bow would swing the other way.

"Steady." We would be upon our old course again.

Once I remember the mate was in the crow's nest and had been narrowly missing ice all day for the fun of the thing—"showing off," as we rather disturbed green hands said. A berg about thirty feet high, a giant for Bering Sea waters, showed a little ahead and to leeward of our course. The mate thought he could pass to windward. He kept the brig close to the wind until the berg was very near. Then he saw a windward passage was impossible and tried suddenly to go to leeward.

"Hard up your wheel," he cried.

"Hard up it is, sir."

The bow swung toward the berg—swung slowly, slowly across it. The tip of the jib-boom almost rammed a white pinnacle. Just when everybody was expecting the brig to pile up in wreck on the ice, the great berg swept past our starboard rail. But we had not missed it. Its jagged edges scraped a line an inch deep along our side from bow to stern.

Shooting *okchug* (or, as it is sometimes spelled, ooksook) or hair seals was a favorite amusement in the spring ice. The mate was an expert with a rifle. He shot many as they lay sunning themselves on ice cakes. Okchugs are as large as oxen and are covered with short silvery hair so glossy that it fairly sparkles. If an okchug was killed outright, its head dropped over upon the ice and it lay still. If only slightly wounded, the animal flounced off into the sea. If vitally hurt, it remained motionless with its head up and glaring defiance, whereupon a boat's crew would row out to the ice cake and a sailor would finish the creature with a club.

It was exciting to step on a small ice cake to face a wounded and savage okchug. The animal would come bouncing on its flippers straight at one with a vicious barking roar. The nose was the okchug's most vulnerable point. A tap on the nose with a club would stretch the great creature out dead. It required a cool head, a steady nerve, and a good aim to deliver this finishing stroke upon the small black snout. If one missed or slipped on the ice, the possible consequences would not have been pleasant. We tanned the skins of the okchugs and made them into trousers or "pokes." The meat was hung over the bows to keep in an ice-box of all outdoors. Ground up and made into sausages, it was a *pièce de resistance* on the forecastle bill of fare.

One night in the latter part of May we saw far off a great light flaring smokily across the sea. It was what is known in whaler parlance as a bug-light and was made by blazing blubber swinging in an iron basket between the two smokestacks of a whale ship's try-works. By it the crew of that distant ship was working at trying out a whale. The bug-light signaled to all the whaling fleet the first whale of the season.

The great continent of ice drifting southward gradually closed round the fleet. The ships had worked so far in there was no escape. In the early part of June the brig was frozen in. For three weeks the vessel remained motionless in solid ice with every stitch of canvas furled. No water or land was in sight—nothing but one great sweep of broken and tumbled ice as far as the eye could see. Those three ice-bound June weeks were given over to idleness. A stove was placed in the forecastle and was kept going night and day. This made it possible to keep comfortable and to read.

We went on frequent seal hunts. We strolled across the frozen sea to visit the other ships, the nearest of which was two miles away. Visiting is called "gamming" by whalers. We learned the gossip of the fleet, who had taken the first whale, how many whales had been caught, the adventures of the ships, the comedies and tragedies of the whaling season.

We established, too, what we called the "Bering Sea Circulating Library." There were a number of books in every forecastle. These greasy, dog-eared volumes were passed about from ship to ship. Perhaps there were twenty books aboard the brig which had been read by almost every member of the crew, forward and aft. Before we got out of the ice, we had exchanged these volumes for an entirely new lot from other ships.

One morning I awoke with the ship rocking like a cradle. I pulled on my clothes and hurried on deck. The ice fields were in wild commotion. Great swells from some storm upon the open sea to the south were rolling under them. Crowded and tumultuous waves of ice twenty feet high chased each other across the frozen fields from horizon to horizon. The ship would sink for a moment between ridges of ice and snow, and then swing up on the crest of an ice mountain. Great areas of ice would fall away as if the sea had opened beneath them. Then they would shoot up and shut out half the sky.

The broken and jagged edges of these white and solid billows appeared for an instant like a range of snowy sierras which, in another instant, would crumble from view as if some seismic cataclysm had shaken them down in ruin. The air was filled with grinding, crushing, ominous noises and explosions.

The ship was in imminent peril. In that mad turmoil of ice it seemed certain she would be ground to pieces. Captain Shorey, who was hobbling about on crutches, ordered a cask of bread, a cask of water, and a barrel of beef hoisted on deck ready to be thrown out on an ice cake in case the brig were wrecked and we were cast away.

In the grinding of the floes, the ship became wedged in between two immense pieces of ice. The great bergs washed closer and closer. When they rose on some tremendous billow, great caverns, washed out by the sea, appeared in their sides like mouths, edged with splinters and points of blue and glittering ice, like fangs. As they rose and fell, it seemed the two white monsters were opening and closing devouring maws for us while the suck of the water in their ice caves made noises like the roar of hungry beasts of prey.

A cable was run out hurriedly over the bow and a bowline at the end of it was slipped over a hummock of ice. With the inboard end wound around the windlass, all hands worked like beavers to heave the brig out of her dangerous position. It was all the crew could do to swing the windlass bars up and down. The ship went forward slowly, almost imperceptibly, and all the time the great bergs swept closer and closer. For a long time it looked as if we were doomed. There was no doubt about the ship's fate if the bergs struck it. But inch by inch, heave by heave, we hauled her through. Ten minutes later, the ice monsters came together with a force that would have crushed an ironclad.

Gradually patches of clear water began to appear in the ice. It was as though the white fields were opening great blue eyes. Little lakes and zigzag lanes of water formed. Sails were set. The brig began to work her way along. Soon she was swinging on heavy billows—not white billows of ice but green billows of water, thick with ice in stars and constellations.

11

Cross Country Whaling

WE had hardly washed clear of the ice in the heavy seas when "Blow!" rang from the crow's nest. A school of whales close ahead, covering the sea with fountains, was coming leisurely toward the ship. There were more than thirty of them.

"Bowheads!" shouted the mate.

Their great black heads rose above the surface like ponderous pieces of machinery; tall fountains shot into the air; the wind caught the tops of the fountains and whisked them off in smoke; hollow, sepulchral whispers of sound came to the brig as the breath left the giant lungs in mighty exhalations. Why they were called bowheads was instantly apparent—the outline of the top of the head curved like an Indian's bow. As the head sank beneath the surface, the glistening back, half as broad as a city street and as black as asphalt, came spinning up out of the sea and went spinning down again.

Our crippled captain in his fur clothes and on crutches limped excitedly about the quarter-deck glaring at $300,000 worth of whales spouting under his nose. But with so much ice about and such a heavy sea running he was afraid to lower.

If the whales saw the brig they gave no sign. They passed all around the vessel, the spray of their fountains blowing on deck. One headed straight for the ship. The mate seized a shoulder bomb-gun and ran to the bow. The whale rose, blew a fountain up against the jib-boom, and dived directly beneath the brig's forefoot. As its back curled down, the mate, with one knee resting on the starboard knighthead, took aim and fired. He surely hit the whale—there was little chance to miss. But the bomb evidently did not strike a vital spot, for the leviathan passed under the ship, came up on the other side and went on about its business.

The sight of all these whales passing by us with such unconcern, blowing water on us as if in huge contempt, almost seeming to laugh at us and mock our bombs and harpoons and human skill, drove the captain frantic. Should he allow that fortune in whales to escape him without a try for it? With purple face and popping eyes he gazed at the herd now passing astern.

"Lower them boats!" he cried.

"What?" expostulated Mr. Landers. "Do you want to get us all killed?"

"Lower them boats!" yelled the skipper.

"Don't you know that a boat that gets fast to a whale in that ice will be smashed, sure?"

"Lower them boats!" shouted the captain.

Mr. Winchester, enthusiastic and fearless whaleman that he was, was eager for the captain's order. His boat and Mr. Landers's went down. The waist boat—mine—was left on its davits. But Gabriel, its boatheader, armed with a shoulder gun, went in the mate's boat. Left aboard to help work ship, I had an opportunity to view that exciting chase from beginning to end.

With storm-reefed sails, the boats went plunging away over the big seas, dodging sharply about to avoid the ice cakes. Not more than two hundred yards away on our starboard beam a great whale was blowing. The mate marked it and went for it like a bull dog. He steered to intercept its course. It was a pretty piece of maneuvering. The whale rose almost in front of him and his boat went shooting upon its back. Long John let fly his harpoon. Gabriel fired a bomb from his shoulder gun. There was a flurry of water as the whale plunged under. Back and forth it slapped with its mighty flukes as it disappeared, narrowly missing the boat. Down came the boat's sail. It was bundled up in a jiffy and the mast slewed aft until it stuck out far behind. Out went the sweeps. The mate stood in the stern wielding a long steering oar. I could see the whale line whipping and sizzling out over the bows.

For only a moment the whale remained beneath the surface. Then it breached. Its black head came shooting up from the water like a titanic rocket. Up went the great body into the air until at least forty feet of it was lifted against the sky like some weird, mighty column, its black sides glistening and its belly showing white. Then the giant bulk crashed down again with a smack on the sea that might have been heard for miles and an impact that sent tons of water splashing high in the air. For an instant the monster labored on the water as if mortally hurt, spouting up fountains of clotted blood that splattered over the ice blocks and turned them from snow white to crimson. Then a second time the whale sounded and went speeding away to windward, heading for the ice pack.

It dragged the boat at a dizzy clip despite the fact that the line was running out so fast as to seem to the men in the boat a mere vibrant, indistinct smear of yellow. The boat was taken slicing through the big waves, driving its nose at times beneath the water, and knocking against lumps of ice. A long ice block appeared in its course. A collision seemed inevitable unless the boat was cut loose from the whale.

Captain Shorey was watching the chase with fierce intentness as he leaned upon his crutches on the forecastle head. He had been filled with great joy, seized with anxiety or shaken with anger as the hunt passed from one phase to another. He shouted his emotions aloud though there was never a chance for the men in the boats to hear him.

"Good boy, Long John," he had cried when the boat-steerer drove his harpoon home.

"That's our fish," he had chortled as the wounded leviathan leaped high against the sky and spouted blood over the ice.

Now when it seemed possible that the mate would be forced to cut loose from the whale to save his boat from destruction, the captain danced about on his crutches in wild excitement.

"Don't cut that line! Don't cut that line!" he yelled.

Mr. Winchester realized as well as the captain that there was something like $10,000 on the other end of the rope, and he had no idea of cutting loose. Towed by the whale the boat drove toward the ice. The mate worked hard with his steering oar to avoid striking the block. It was impossible. The bow smashed into one end of the ice cake, was lifted out of the water and dragged across to slip back into the sea. A hole was stove in the starboard bow through which the water rushed. The crew thereafter was kept busy bailing.

It was evident from the fountains of blood that the whale was desperately wounded, but its vitality was marvelous and it seemed it might escape. When Mr. Landers saw the mate's line being played out so rapidly he should have hurried to the mate's boat and bent the line from his own tub to the end of the mate's line. As an old whaleman Mr. Landers knew what to do in this crisis, but in such ice and in such high seas he preferred not to take a chance. He was a cautious soul, so he held his boat aloof. The mate waved to him frantically. Long John and Gabriel wigwagged frenzied messages with waving arms.

As for Captain Shorey on his crutches on the forecastle head, when it seemed certain that the whale would run away with all the mate's line and escape, he apparently suffered temporary aberration. He damned old man Landers in every picturesque and fervent term of an old whaleman's vocabulary. He shook his fist at him. He waved a crutch wildly.

"Catch that whale!" he yelled in a voice husky and broken with emotion. "For God's sake, catch that whale!"

All this dynamic pantomime perhaps had its effect on Landers. At any rate, his men began to bend to their sweeps and soon his boat was alongside that of the mate. His line was tied to the free end of the rope in the mate's almost exhausted tub just in time. The mate's line ran out and Landers's boat now became fast to the whale.

Fortune favored Landers. His boat was dragged over the crests of the seas at thrilling speed, but he managed to keep clear of ice. The whale showed no sign of slowing down. In a little while it had carried away all the line in Mr. Landers's tub. The monster was free of the boats at last. It had ceased to come to the surface to blow. It had gone down into the deep waters carrying with it the mate's harpoon and 800 fathoms of manila rope. It seemed probable it had reached the safety of the ice pack and was lost.

The boats came back to the brig; slowly, wounded, limping over the waves. The flying spray had frozen white over the fur clothes of the men, making them look like snow images. They climbed aboard in silence. Mr. Landers had a hang-dog, guilty look. The skipper was a picture of gloom and smoldering fury. He bent a black regard upon Mr. Landers as the latter swung over the rail, but surprised us all by saying not a word.

When the next day dawned, we were out of sight of ice, cruising in a quiet sea. A lookout posted on the forecastle head saw far ahead a cloud of gulls flapping about a dark object floating on the surface. It was the dead whale.

12

Cutting In and Trying Out

TWO boats were sent to secure the whale. I lowered with one. As we came up to the whale, I marveled at its immense bulk. It looked even larger than when it had breached and I had seen it shoot up, a giant column of flesh and blood, against the heavens. It had turned belly up as dead whales do, its ridged white abdomen projecting above the waves. It seemed much like a mighty white and black rock, against which the waves lapped lazily. Seventy-five feet long the officers estimated it—an unusually large bull whale. I had never imagined any animal so large. I had seen Jumbo, said to be the largest elephant ever in captivity. Jumbo made ordinary circus elephants seem like pigmies. This whale was as big as a dozen Jumbos. The great hairy mammoth, of which I had seen stuffed specimens in museums, would have seemed a mere baby beside this monster of the deep.

As proof that the whale was ours, the harpoon sticking in its back bore the brig's name, and fast to the haft and floating far out on the sea in a tangled mass was the 800 fathoms of line from the brig's two tubs. Our first work was to recover the line. As this had to be straightened out and coiled in the boats, it was a long and tedious job. Then with a short sharp spade, a hole was cut through the whale's flukes and a cable passed through and made fast. With both boats strung out along the cable, the men bent to the sweeps, hauling the carcass slowly toward the brig. Meanwhile the vessel had been sailing toward us. So we had but a hundred yards or so to pull.

The loose end of the hawser was passed through the hawse hole in the starboard bow and made fast to the fore-bitt. In this way the flukes were held close to the bow. As the brig made headway under short sail, the great body washed back against the vessel's side and lay upon the surface, the head abreast the wheel on the quarter-deck—which will give an idea of the whale's length.

The gang-plank was taken from the bulwarks and a cutting stage lowered over the whale. This stage was made of three broad planks. Two projected from the ship's side, the third joined their outer ends. Along the inside of the third plank was a low railing. Two officers took their station on the outer plank with long-handled spades to cut in the blubber. The spade was enough like a garden spade in shape to suggest its name and was fastened to a long pole. Its cutting edge was as sharp as a razor.

A block and tackle was rigged above the whale, the upper block fastened to the cross-trees of the main mast and the tackle carried forward to the windlass. A great hook was fastened into the whale's blubber, and every-thing was ready for the cutting in.

As the officers with their spades cut under the blubber, the sailors heaved on the windlass. The blanket piece of blubber began to rise. As it rose, the officers kept spading under it, rolling the whale over gradually. Thus the whale was peeled much as one would peel a roll of bologna sausage. When the great carcass had been rolled completely over, the blanket piece of blubber came off. The upper end of it fast to the tackle hook was up almost against the cross-trees as the lower end swung free. The largest blanket pieces weighed perhaps ten tons. Six were taken off in the process of skinning. The weight of the whale,

I should estimate, was roughly something like one hundred tons, perhaps a little more.

When the blanket piece was cut free from the whale it swung inboard, and as it came over the main hatch, it was lowered into the hold. There men fell upon it with short spades, cutting it into small pieces and distributing them equally about the ship to prevent the vessel from listing. It took most of the day to strip the whale of its blubber. When this had been finished the great flensed carcass stretched out along the ship's side a mass of blood-red flesh. The final work was cutting in the "old head."

Long John with an axe climbed down upon the whale's back. As it was his boat that had struck the whale the cutting in of the head was his job. Nobody envied him the task. The stripped body of a whale offers a surface as slippery as ice. As the waves rocked the whale, Long John had much ado to keep his footing. Once he fell and almost tumbled into the water. Finally he cut himself two foot-holds and began to wield his axe, raining blows upon the neck. He chopped through from the upper neck surface into the corners of the mouth, thus loosening the head and upper jaw from the body. The lower jaw is devoid of teeth. The tackle hook having been fixed in the tip-top of the head's bowlike curve, the windlass men heaved away. Up rose the head above the bulwarks and swung inwards.

"Lower, lower away!" cried the mate.

Down came the head upon the deck and a great cheer went up. The "old head" was safe. Immediately afterwards, the mate came forward with a bottle of Jamaica rum and gave each man a swig. "Bringing in his old head," as it is called, is a memorable event in cutting in a whale, and is always celebrated by dealing out a drink all around.

Great hunks of meat were cut out from the carcass. These were hung over the bow. The meat was served in the form of steaks and sausages in both forecastle and cabin. And let me give my testimony right here that whale steak is mighty good eating. It tastes something like tender beef, though it is coarser grained and of ranker flavor. We preferred to eat it as steaks, though made into meat balls with gravy it was extremely toothsome. I do not know how whale would taste if served on the home table, but at sea, after months of salt horse and "sow belly," it was delicious. The hunks became coated with ice over the bow and kept well. They lasted us for several weeks.

When the carcass was cut adrift it went floating astern. Flocks of gulls and sea birds that had been constantly hovering about the ship in hundreds waiting for the feast swooped down upon it. The body washed slowly out of sight, still swarmed over by the gulls.

The head rested in the waist near the poop. It was, I should say, twelve feet high at the crest of the bow, and suggested some strange sort of tent. I stepped inside it without bending my head and walked about in it. Its sides were shaggy with the long hair hanging from the teeth or baleen, and the interior resembled, in a way, a hunter's forest lodge made of pine boughs. If the head had been in a forest instead of on the deck of a ship it would have formed an ideal shelter for a winter's night with a wood fire burning at the opening.

Only the lower tip of the head or what we might call the nose rested on the deck. It was supported otherwise upon the teeth. I now had my first opportunity to see baleen in its natural setting. The teeth viewed from the outside looked something like the interior of a piano. The whale's gums, following the bony skeleton of the jaw, formed an arched and undulant line from nose tip to the back of the jaw. The front teeth were six inches long; the back ones were ten feet. Each tooth, big and little alike, was formed of a thin slab of bluish whalebone, almost flat. The largest of these slabs were six inches broad at their base in the gum. The smallest were an inch. All tapered to a point. They were set in the gum with the flat surfaces together and almost touching. They were extremely pliant and at the outer ends could be pulled wide apart. The inner edges were hung with black coarse hair, which seemed exactly like that of a horse's tail. The hair on the small front teeth was an inch long perhaps; on the back teeth, it was from six to ten inches long.

Such teeth are beautifully adapted to the animal's feeding habits. The baleen whale feeds on a kind of jelly fish. We saw at times the sea covered with these flat, round, whitish living discs. The whale swims through an area of this food with its mouth open. When it has obtained a mouthful, it closes its jaws. The water is forced out between the slab-like teeth; the jelly fish remain tangled in the hair to be gulped down.

Our first job after the cutting in of the whale was to cut the baleen from the jaw. It was cut away in bunches of ten or a dozen slabs held together by the gums and stowed away in the hold not to be touched again until later in the voyage.

While the baleen was being prepared for stowage, the lid was removed from the try-works, uncovering the two big copper caldrons.

A fire was started in the furnace with kindling and a handful of coal, but kept going thereafter with tried-out blubber called "scrap." Two men dressed in oil-skins were sent down into the blubber-room as the portion of the hold was called in which the blanket pieces of blubber had been stowed. Their oil-skins were to protect them from the oil which oozed from the blubber. Oil-skins, however, are but slight protection as I learned later when I was sent into the blubber room at the taking of another whale. The oil soaks through the water-proof oil-skins and saturates one's clothes and goes clear through to the skin leaving it as greasy as if it had been rubbed with oil.

A whale's blubber lies immediately beneath its skin, which is black and rubbery and about a quarter of an inch thick. The blubber is packed between this thin covering and the flesh in a layer of pink and opalescent fat from six inches to two feet thick. The blubber is so full of oil that the oil exudes from it. One can squeeze the oil from a piece of raw blubber as water from a sponge.

The two blubber-room men with short handled spades cut the great blankets of blubber in what in whaling parlance are called "horse pieces." These horse pieces are two or three feet long and about six inches wide. They are pitched into tubs on deck and the tubs dragged forward to the mincing vat. This is an immense oblong tub across the top of which is fastened a plank. Two sailors with mincing knives are stationed at each end of the plank. The mincing knife is like a carpenter's drawing knife, except that the edge is on the outside. The sailor lays a horse piece along the plank. Then grasping the mincing knife by its two handles, he passes the blade back and forth from side to side across the blubber until it has been cut into leaves something like those of a book, each leaf perhaps a quarter of an inch thick and all of them held together at the back by the black skin. Thus minced the horse pieces are pitch-forked into the caldrons that are kept bubbling with boiling oil. When the oil has been boiled out of them, the horse-pieces, now shrunken and twisted into hard, brittle lumps, called "scrap," are skimmed off and thrown into a vat at the port side of the try-works to be used later as fuel in trying out the remainder of the blubber. The oil is ladled off into a cooling vat at the starboard side where, after it has cooled, it is siphoned into hogsheads or tanks and these are later stowed in the hold.

The trying out of the whale gave several delicacies to the forecastle menu. Hardtack biscuit soaked in buckets of sea water and then boiled in the bubbling caldrons of oil made relishing morsels. The crisp, tried-out blubber, which looked like honey-comb, was palatable to some. Black whale skin freed of blubber and cut into small cubes and pickled in salt and vinegar had a rather agreeable taste, though it was much like eating pickled rubber. These things with whale steaks and whale sausages made trying-out days a season of continual feasting.

At night "scrap" was put into an iron basket swung between the two chimneys of the try-works and set on fire, making a flaring yellow blaze which lighted the ship from stem to stern and threw weird shadows everywhere. The beacon not only gave us plenty of light to work by, but advertised the brig's good luck to any ship which happened in sight of us. In the blubber-room, holes were cut in a blanket piece and rope yarns, having been rubbed upon the blubber, were coiled in the hole and lighted. As they burned they lighted the oil from the blubber. These unique lamps had all the oil in a ten-ton blanket piece to draw on. It was only the wick that ever gave out. New strands of rope yarn had to be provided from time to time. Three or four of these lamps blazing and spluttering made the blubber-room bright.

Working night and day, it took three days to cut in and try out the whale. While the work was going on, the decks were so greasy that we could run and slide anywhere for long distances like boys on ice. After the whale had been tried out and the oil casks had been stowed below, we fell upon the decks and paint work with lye and water. Hard work soon had the ship looking as bright as a new pin.

13

Shaking Hands
with Siberia

THE ship's prow was turned northward after work on the whale had been finished. I expected we would soon run into the ice again. We sailed on and on, but not a block of ice big enough to make a highball did we sight. The white floes and drifts and the frozen continent floating southward, along the coasts of which we had cruised for whales and which had surrounded us and held us captive for three weeks, had disappeared entirely. The warm water from the south, the southern winds, and the spring sunshine had melted the ice. Its utter disappearance savored of magic.

A long hilly coast rose ahead of us covered with grass, barren of trees or shrubs, dotted with blackened skeletons of old ice—an utterly desolate land. It was Siberia. We put into a bight called St. Lawrence Bay. There was an Eskimo village on the shore. The huts were made of whale ribs covered with hides of walrus and reindeer. In the warm weather, some of the hides had been removed and we saw the white gleaming bones of the frame work. We could see the dogs with tails curling over their backs frisking about and could hear their clamor as they bayed at the great white-winged thing that had come up from over the sea's verge.

In this first part of July it was continuous day. The sun set at eleven o'clock at night in the northwest. Its disc remained barely below the horizon—we could almost see its flaming rim. A molten glow of color made the sky resplendent just above it as it passed across the north pole. It rose at 1:30 in the morning high in the northeast. All the time it was down a brilliant twilight prevailed—a twilight like that which in our temperate zone immediately follows the sinking of the sun behind a hill. We could see to read without difficulty.

Soon boats and kayaks were putting off from the village. When we were still a mile or two out, strange craft came alongside and Eskimo men, women, and children swarmed aboard. Very picturesque they looked in clothes made of the skins of reindeer, hair seals, dogs, and squirrels, oddly trimmed and decorated with fur mosaics in queer designs. Some of the women wore over their furs a yellow waterproof cloak made of the intestines of fish, ornamented with needle-work figures and quite neat looking.

The men and the older women had animal faces of low intelligence. The young girls were extremely pretty, with glossy, coal-black hair, bright black eyes, red cheeks, lips like ripe cherries, and gleaming white teeth forever showing in the laughter of irresponsibility and perfect health.

The captain ordered a bucket of hardtack brought out in honor of our guests. The biscuit were dumped in a pile on the main deck. The Eskimos gathered around in a solemn and dignified circle. The old men divided the bread, giving an equal number of hardtack to each.

This ceremony of welcome over, the Eskimos were given the freedom of the ship, or at least, took it. We kept a careful watch upon them, however, to see that they took nothing else. Several of the Eskimo men had a suffi-cient smattering of English to make themselves understood. They had picked up their small vocabulary among the whalers which every spring put in at the little ports along the Siberian and Alaskan coasts. One of them had been whaling to the Arctic Ocean aboard a whale ship which some accident had left short handed. He spoke better English than any of the others and was evidently regarded by his fellow townsmen as a wonderfully intellectual person. He became quite friendly with me, showing his friendship by begging me to give him almost everything I had, from tobacco to clothes. He constantly used an Eskimo word the meaning of which all whalers have learned and it assisted him materially in telling his stories—he was a great story teller. This word was "pau"—it means "nothing." I never knew before how important nothing could be in human language. Here is a sample of his use of "nothing:"

"Winter," he said, "sun pau; daylight pau. All dark. Water pau; all ice. Land pau, all snow. Eskimo igloo, plenty fire. Moss in blubber oil all time blaze up. Cold pau. Plenty hot. Eskimo, he sweat. Clothes pau. Good time. Hot time. Eat plenty. Sleep."

This seemed to me a good, vivid description. The picture was there, painted chiefly with "nothing."

Of course he had the English words "yes" and "no" in his assortment, but his way of using them was pure Eskimo. For instance:

"You wear no clothes in winter?" I asked him.

"No," he replied.

"No?" I echoed in surprise.

"Yes," he said. His "yes" merely affirmed his "no." It sometimes required a devious mental process to follow him.

A pretty girl came up to me with a smile and an ingratiating air.

"Tobac," she said holding out her hand.

I handed her my smoking plug. She took half of it at one cavernous bite and gave the remainder back to me, which I thought considerate. She enjoyed the tobacco. She chewed upon it hard, working her jaws as if she were masticating a dainty tidbit. Did she expectorate? Not a drop. She evidently did not propose to waste any of the flavor of that good weed. Neither did she get sick—that pretty Eskimo girl. At last when she had chewed for twenty minutes or so, she removed her quid and stuck it behind her right ear. She chewed it at intervals later on, always between times wearing it conspicuously behind her ear.

I rather expected our guests would depart after a call of an hour or so. Not so. They had come to stay indefinitely. When they became tired they lay on deck—it didn't make any particular difference where—and went quietly to sleep. They seemed to have no regular time for sleeping. I found Eskimos asleep and awake during all my deck watches. As it was day all the twenty-four hours, I wondered if these people without chronometers did not sometimes get their hours mixed up.

New parties of Eskimos kept coming to see us. One of these had killed a walrus and the skin and the raw meat, butchered into portable cuts, lay in the bottom of their big family canoe of hide. The boat was tied alongside and the Eskimos came aboard. If any of them became hungry, they climbed down into the canoe and ate the raw walrus meat, smacking their lips over it. When the sailors would lean over the rail to watch this strange feat of gastronomy, the Eskimos would smile up at them with mouths smeared with blood and hold out a red chunk in invitation. It was their joke.

We loafed in St. Lawrence Bay for more than a week. We could not have sailed away if we had wanted to, for all the time there was a windless calm and the sea heaved and fell, unruffled by a ripple, like a vast sheet of moving mercury. It was weather characteristic of the Arctic summer—a beautiful dream season of halcyon, silver seas, opalescent haze, and tempered golden sunlight. To the men in skin clothes, it was warm weather, but one had only to step from sunshine to shadow to pass from summer to winter. One perspired in the sunlight; in the shadow there was frost, and if the spot were damp, a coating of ice.

I went duck hunting with a boat's crew one day. Mr. Winchester, who headed the boat, was a good hand with a shotgun and brought back a fine bag. One of the ducks, knocked over on the wing, dropped within a few feet of shore. When we rowed to pick it up, I touched Siberia with an oar. I felt that it was a sort of handshake with the Asiatic continent. I never landed and never got any nearer.

In a little while, most of us had traded for a number of nicely tanned hair-seal skins and had set the Eskimo women and girls to work tailoring trousers and vests and coats. It was marvelous how dexterous they were at cutting and sewing. They took no measurements and yet their garments fitted rather snugly. Before they began sewing they softened the edges of the skins by chewing them. They wore their thimble on their index finger and drove the needle into one side of the skins and jerked it through from the other side with such amazing rapidity that the two movements seemed one. A good seamstress—and all seemed remarkably expert—could cut and sew a pair of trousers in an hour, a bit of work it would have taken a sailor a day or two to accomplish. We could hire a seamstress for an entire morning or afternoon for five hardtack. A bowl of soup with a piece of salt horse was sufficient pay for a day's labor.

My old skin clothes, which I had obtained from the slop-chest were greasy, dirty, and worn and I had an Eskimo woman make me a complete new outfit from hair-seal skins I purchased from her husband. She cut out a coat, vest, and trousers, spreading the skins on deck and using a knife in cutting. She sat cross-legged on deck most of the day sewing on the garments and I carefully superintended the job, She ornamented the coat with a black dogskin collar and edged it down the breast and around the bottom with the same material, which set off the glistening seal skin attractively. I also bought a new squirrel skin shirt with a hood attached. When I appeared on deck in my new toggery, I felt quite presentable.

However, I was not alone in gorgeous regalia. Most of my shipmates were soon looking like animate statues of silver in their shining seal skins. Our turns up and down deck became fashion parades. We strutted like peacocks, it must be admitted, and displayed our fine clothes to best advantage under the eyes of the Eskimo beauties.

It remained for Peter, our roly-poly little Swede, to make the only real, simon-pure conquest. In his new clothes, which sparkled like a silver dollar fresh from the mint, and with his fresh boyish face, he cut quite a handsome figure and one little Eskimo maid fell a victim to his fatal fascinations.

"'E's killed her dead," said English Bill White.

She was perhaps fifteen years old, roguish eyed, rosy cheeked, and with coal-black hair parted in the middle and falling in two braids at the sides of her head. Plump and full of life and high spirits, the gay little creature was as pretty as any girl I saw among the Eskimos.

Peter was all devotion. He gave his sweetheart the lion's share of all his meals, feasting her on salt horse, hardtack, soup, and gingerbread which to her primitive palate that never had risen to greater gastronomic heights than blubber and raw meat must have seemed epicurean delicacies.

The sailors called the girl "Mamie," which was very different from the Eskimo name her mother spluttered at her. If Peter was missed at any time, it was only necessary to locate the charming Miss Mamie, and there by her side

Peter would be found, speaking only with his eyes and making distinct progress.

Sometimes Peter, finding optical language not entirely satisfactory, pressed into his service the intellectual Eskimo as interpreter. These three-cornered efforts at love making were amusing to all who chanced to overhear them— the dashing young Romeo could scarcely talk English himself, the interpreter could talk even less and the object of Peter's adoration could not speak a word.

As the upshot of this interesting affair, the little lady and Peter plotted between them that Peter should run away from the ship and live among her people. This plan appealed to Peter who was a cold weather product himself and almost as primitive as his inamorata. But Peter made one mistake—he took old Nels Nelson, his countryman and side-partner, into his confidence. Nelson loved the boy like a father and did his best to persuade him to give up the idea, but Peter was determined.

One twilight midnight with the sun just skimming below the horizon, Peter wrapped from head to foot in an Eskimo woman's mackintosh of fish intestine, with the hood over his head and half hiding his chubby face, climbed over the rail into an Eskimo boat with a number of natives, his sweetheart among them, and set out for shore. Nelson and several sailors watched the boat paddle away, but no one but Nelson knew that the person bundled up in the native raincoat was Peter. The boat got half a mile from the brig. Then Nelson could stand it no longer. The strain was too much. He rushed back to the quarter-deck where old Gabriel was walking up and down.

"Peter's run away," Nelson blurted out. "There he goes in that boat. That's him dressed up like a woman in fish-gut oil-skins."

Without ado Gabriel called aft the watch, manned a boat, and set out in pursuit. The Eskimo canoe was quickly overhauled and Peter was captured and brought back aboard.

"You ben bigges' fool for sech a lil' boy I ever have see," said Gabriel severely. "You don't know you freeze to deaf up here in winter time, no?"

Peter had nothing to say. He was ashamed, but he was mad, too. He was not punished. When Captain Shorey learned of the escapade, he merely laughed. Peter took the matter quite to heart and pouted for days. To the end of the voyage, he still dreamed of his Eskimo sweetheart and of the happiness that might have been his. Every time he spoke of her his eyes grew bright. "She was fine gal," he used to say.

14

Moonshine and Hygiene

WE noticed that several of our Eskimo guests appeared at times to be slightly under the influence of liquor and thought perhaps they had obtained gin or rum from some whaling vessel that had touched at the port before we arrived. We asked the intellectual Eskimo where these fellows had got their booze. He pointed to an Eskimo and said, "Him."

"Him" was a lordly person dressed in elaborately trimmed and ornamented skin clothes. From the way he strutted about, we had fancied him a chief. He turned out to be a "moonshiner."

This doubtless will surprise those whose ideas of "moonshiners" are associated with southern Appalachian ranges, lonely mountain coves, revenue raids, and romance. But here was an Eskimo "moonshiner" who made unlicensed whiskey under the midnight sun and yet was as genuine a "moonshiner" as any lawless southern mountaineer. The sailors, being thirsty souls, at once opened negotiations with him for liquor. He drew from beneath his deer-skin coat a skin bottle filled with liquor and sold it to us for fifteen hardtack. Wherefore there was, for a time, joy in the forecastle—in limited quantity, for the bottle was small. This product of the icebound North was the hottest stuff I ever tasted.

The captain was not long in discovering that the Eskimo had liquor to sell and sent a boat ashore with a demijohn. The jug was brought back filled with Siberian "moonshine," which had been paid for with a sack of flour. The boat's crew found on the beach a little distillery in comparison with which the pot stills of the Kentucky and Tennessee mountains, made of old kitchen kettles would seem elaborate and up-to-date plants. The still itself was an old tin oil can; the worm, a twisted gun barrel; the flake-stand, a small powder keg. The mash used in making the liquor, we learned, was a fermented mixture of flour and molasses obtained in trade from whale ships. It was boiled in the still, a twist of moss blazing in a pan of blubber oil doing duty as a furnace. The vapor from the boiling mash passed through the worm in the flake-stand and was condensed by ice-cold water with which the powder keg was kept constantly filled by hand. The liquor dripped from the worm into a battered old tomato can. It was called "kootch" and was potently intoxicating. An Eskimo drunk on "kootch" was said to be brave enough to tackle a polar bear, single-handed. The little still was operated in full view of the villagers. There was no need of secrecy, Siberia boasted no revenue raiders.

The owner of the plant did an extensive trade up and down the coast and it was said natives from Diomede Islands and Alaska paddled over in their canoes and *bidarkas* to buy his liquor. They paid for it in walrus tusk ivory, whale bone, and skins and the "moonshiner" was the richest man in all that part of Siberia.

If contact with civilization had taught the Eskimo the art of distillation and drunkenness, it also had improved living conditions among them. Many owned rifles. Their spears and harpoons were steel tipped. They bartered for flour, molasses, sugar, and all kinds of canned goods with the whale ships every summer. They had learned to cook. There was a stove in the village. The intellectual Eskimo boasted of the stove as showing the high degree of civilization achieved by his people. The stove, be it added, was used chiefly for heating purposes in winter and remained idle in summer. The natives regarded the cooked foods of the white man as luxuries to be indulged in only occasionally in a spirit of connoisseurship. They still preferred their immemorial diet of blubber and raw meat.

Aside from these faint touches of civilization, the Eskimos were as primitive in their life and mental processes as people who suddenly had stepped into the present out of the world of ten thousand years ago. I fancy Adam and Eve would have lived after the manner of the Eskimos if the Garden of Eden had been close to the North Pole.

There is apparently no government or law among these Eskimos. They have no chiefs. When it becomes necessary to conduct any business of public importance with outsiders, it is looked after by the old men. The Eskimos are a race, one may say, of individuals. Each one lives his life according to his own ideas; without let or hindrance. Each is a law unto himself. Under these conditions one might expect they would hold to the rule of the strong arm under which might makes right. This is far from true. There is little crime among them. Murder is extremely rare. Though they sometimes steal from white men—the sailors on the brig were warned that they would steal anything not nailed down—they are said never—or hardly ever—to steal from each other. They have a nice respect for the rights of their neighbors. They are not exactly a Golden Rule people, but they mind their own business.

The infrequency of crime among them seems stranger when one learns that they never punish their children. Eskimo children out-Topsy Topsy in "just growing." I was informed that they are never spanked, cuffed, or boxed on the ears. Their little misdemeanors are quietly ignored. It might seem logical to expect these ungoverned and lawless little fellows to grow up into bad men and women. But the ethical tradition of the race holds them straight.

When a crime occurs, the punishment meted out fits it as exactly as possible. We heard of a murder among the Eskimos around St. Lawrence Bay the punishment of which furnishes a typical example of Eskimo justice. A young man years before had slain a missionary by shooting him with a rifle. The old men of the tribe tried the murderer and condemned him to death. His own father executed the sentence with the same rifle with which the missionary had been killed.

Tuberculosis is a greater scourge among the Eskimos than among the peoples of civilization. This was the last disease I expected to find in the cold, pure air of the Arctic region. But I was told that it caused more than fifty per cent of the deaths among the natives. These conditions have been changed for the better within the last few years. School teachers, missionaries, and traveling physicians appointed by the United States government have taught the natives of Alaska hygiene and these have passed on the lesson to their kinsmen of Siberia. Long after my voyage had ended, Captain A.J. Henderson, of the revenue cutter *Thetis* and a pioneer judge of Uncle Sam's "floating court" in Bering Sea and Arctic Ocean waters, told me of the work he had done in spreading abroad the gospel of health among the Eskimos.

Finding tuberculosis carrying off the natives by wholesale, Captain Henderson began the first systematic crusade against the disease during a summer voyage of his vessel in the north. In each village at which the *Thetis* touched, he took the ship's doctor ashore and had him deliver through an interpreter a lecture on tuberculosis. Though the Eskimos lived an out-door life in summer, they shut themselves up in their igloos in winter, venturing out only when necessity compelled them, and living in a super-heated atmosphere without ventilation. As a result their winter igloos became veritable culture beds of the disease.

Those afflicted had no idea what was the matter with them. Their witch doctors believed that they were obsessed by devils and attempted by incantations to exorcise the evil spirits. The doctor of the *Thetis* had difficulty in making the natives understand that the organism that caused their sickness was alive, though invisible. But he did succeed in making them understand that the disease was communicated by indiscriminate expectoration and that prevention and cure lay in plenty of fresh air, cleanliness, and wholesome food.

In all the villages, Captain Henderson found the igloos offensively filthy and garbage and offal scattered about the huts in heaps. He made the Eskimos haul these heaps to sea in boats and dump them overboard. He made them clean their igloos thoroughly and take off the roofs to allow the sun and rains to purify the interiors. After this unroofing, Captain Henderson said, the villages looked as if a cyclone had struck them. He taught the natives how to sew together sputum cups of skin and cautioned the afflicted ones against expectoration except in these receptacles.

The Eskimos were alive to the seriousness of the situation and did their utmost to follow out these hygienic instructions to the last detail. As a result of this first missionary campaign in the cause of health, the Eskimos have begun to keep their igloos clean and to ventilate them in winter. There has grown up among them an unwritten law against indiscriminate expectoration more carefully observed than such ordinances in American cities. The villages have been gradually turned into open-air sanitariums and the death rate from tuberculosis has been materially reduced.

15

News From Home

WITH the first breeze, we set sail for Port Clarence, Alaska, the northern rendezvous of the Arctic Ocean whaling fleet in early summer. There in the latter part of June or the early part of July, the fleet always met the four-masted schooner *Jennie*, the tender from San Francisco, by which all firms in the whaling trade sent mail and supplies to their vessels. On our way across from Siberia to Alaska, we passed just south of Bering Straits and had our first distant glimpse of the Arctic Ocean. When we dropped anchor in the windy roadstead of Port Clarence, eighteen whale ships were there ahead of us.

The land about Port Clarence was flat and covered with tall, rank grass—a region of tundra stretching away to distant hills. The *Jennie* came in direct from San Francisco soon after we arrived. Boats from the whale ships swarmed about her as soon as she dropped anchor, eager for letters and newspapers. Our mate brought back a big bundle of San Francisco newspapers which were sent forward after the cabin had read them. They gave us our first news since leaving Honolulu of how the great world was waging. Every man in the forecastle who could read these papers from the first headline to the last advertisement. It seemed good to get into touch once more with the men and events of civilization. Exiles of the sea, the news of our country seemed to have an intimate personal meaning to us which it never could possibly have to stay-at-homes to whom newspapers are every-day, casual budgets of gossip and information. I remember that a telegraphic brevity describing a murder in my native state seemed like a message from home.

Among the Eskimos who came aboard the brig from the large village on shore, was a white man dressed like an Eskimo to the last detail and looking like one except for a heavy beard. He had run away from a whale ship three years before, hoping to make his way to some white settlement to the south and there secure passage on shipboard back to San Francisco. He had escaped, he said, in an Eskimo kayak tied alongside his ship. As soon as he was missed officers and boat-steerers put ashore in a boat and trailed him. He led his pursuers a long chase inland and though he was shot at several times, he managed to elude them and reach the safety of the hills.

After he had seen the whaling fleet sail away, he ventured back to the Eskimo village on shore where he was welcomed by the natives. He soon found that escape by land was practically impossible; the nearest white settlement was hundreds of miles distant and he would have to thread his way through pathless forests and across ranges of mountains covered at all seasons with ice and snow. Moreover, he learned what he should have known before he ran away that no vessels except whaling ships, their tender, and an occasional revenue cutter ever touched at Port Clarence which at that time was far north of the outmost verge of the world's commerce. There was nothing left for him to do but settle among the Eskimos and wait for the arrival of the whaling fleet in the following summer.

During the long Arctic night, with the temperature forty and fifty degrees below zero, he lived in an igloo after the manner of the natives; learned to eat raw meat and blubber—

there was nothing else to eat—became fluent in the Eskimo language; and took an Eskimo girl for a wife. He found existence among these human anachronisms left over from the stone age a monotonously dreary and soul-wearying experience, and he waited with nervous impatience for the coming of the fleet with its annual opportunity for getting back to civilization.

The first year passed and the ships anchored in Port Clarence. He hurried out in his kayak to ask the captains for permission to work his way back to San Francisco. He never once doubted that they would give him his chance. But a sad surprise was in store for him. From ship to ship he went, begging to be allowed to remain aboard, but the hard-hearted captains coldly refused him, one after the other. He was a deserter, they told him; he had made his bed and he could lie in it; to take him away would encourage others to desert. Some captains cursed him; some ordered him off their vessels. Finally the ships sailed away for the whaling grounds, leaving him marooned on the bleak shore to pass another year in the squalor of his igloo.

Next year when the whaling fleet came again it was the same story over again. Again he watched the ships arrive with a heart beating high with hope and again he saw their topmasts disappear over the horizon, leaving him hopeless and wretched behind. Before he came aboard the brig, he had made the rounds of the other ships and had met with the same refusals as of yore. I saw him go aft and plead with Captain Shorey and that stern old sea dog turned him down as curtly as the other skippers had done. The ships sailed away, leaving him to his fate. To me his story was the most pathetic that ever fell within my personal experience. I never learned whether he ever managed somehow to get back home or left his bones to bleach upon the frozen tundra.

From Port Clarence, we headed back to Unalaska to ship our whale bone to San Francisco by steamer. Midway of our run down the Bering Sea a thick fog closed about us and we kept our fog horn booming. Soon, off our bows, we heard another fog horn. It seemed to be coming closer. Our cooper, an old navy bugler, became suspicious. He got out his old bugle and sounded "assembly" sharply. As the first note struck into the mist, the other fog horn ceased its blowing. We did not hear it again. When the mist lifted, no vessel was in sight, but the situation was clear. We had chanced upon a poaching sealer and when she heard our cooper's bugle, she concluded we were a revenue cutter and took to her heels.

A day or two later, we saw the revenue cutter *Corwin* chasing a poacher. Heeled over under crowded sail, the sealing schooner was scurrying before a stiff wind. The *Corwin* was plowing in hot pursuit, smoke pouring from her funnel and hanging thick in the wake of the chase. She was gaining steadily, for she was a steamship and the schooner had only her sails to depend on. Finally the revenue cutter sent a solid shot across the schooner's bows. The ball knocked up a great splash of water.

But the poacher did not heave to—just kept on her way, leaning so far over that the clews of her lower sails almost touched the waves and a big white feather of spray stood up in front of her. So pursuer and pursued passed over the horizon and we did not see the end of the hunt. But we knew that there could be but one end. The fate of that poacher was sealed. Only a fog could save her, and the sky was clear.

We passed close to St. George Island, the southernmost of the Pribiloff group, the breeding place of the fur seals. As we came near the shores, the air literally shook with the raucous, throbbing bark of countless seals. The din was deafening. Along the shore, a shelving beach ran up to rocky declivities and beach and rocks were packed with seals. There may have been a hundred thousand; there may have been a million; and it seemed as if every seal was barking. The water alongshore swarmed with them. Thousands of heads were sticking out of the sea. Thousands of other seals were playing, breaching out of the water like porpoises. They swam close to the brig and floated lazily on the surface, staring at us unafraid. If we had been poachers, I should think we could have taken several hundred thousand dollars worth of seals without difficulty.

A dozen little pup seals whose fur was of a snowy and unspotted white came swimming about the vessel. These sea babies were soft, furry, cunning little fellows and they paddled about the brig, sniffing at the strange monster that had invaded their home. They seemed absolutely fearless and gazed up at us out of big, brown, wondering, friendly eyes. Sealers kill them, as their fur makes beautiful edgings and borders for fur garments.

The fur seals are supposed to pass the winter somewhere in the South Pacific, but whether in the open sea or on land has never been definitely learned. From their mysterious southern hiding places, they set out for the North in the early spring. They first appear in March in the waters off California. Coastwise vessels find the sea alive with thousands of them. They travel slowly northward following the coast line, fifty or a hundred miles out at sea, feeding on fish and sleeping on the surface. Regularly each year in April, a revenue cutter setting out from Port Townsend for patrol service in Bering Sea and Arctic Ocean waters, picks up the herd and convoys it to the Pribiloffs to guard it against the attacks of poachers. The seals swarm through the passes between the Aleutian Islands in May and arrive at the Pribiloffs in the latter part of that month or early in June.

They remain on the Pribiloffs during the breeding and rearing season and begin to depart for the South again in the latter part of September. They are all gone as a rule by November, though in some years the last ones do not leave until December. They are again seen as they crowd through the Aleutian channels, but all track of them is lost a few hundred miles to the south. At what destination they finally arrive on that southward exodus no man knows. It is one of the mysteries of the sea.

We saw no whales on our southward passage and did not much expect to see any, though we kept a lookout at the mast-head on the off chance of sighting some lone spout. The summer months are a second "between seasons," dividing the spring whaling in Bering Sea from that in the Arctic Ocean in the fall. The whales had all followed the retreating ice northward through Bering Straits.

The Fourth of July found us in the middle of Bering Sea. We observed the glorious Fourth by hoisting the American flag to our gaff-topsail peak, where it fluttered all day long. Mr. Winchester came forward with two bottles of Jamaica rum and dealt out a drink all around.

We entered Unalaska Harbor by the same long, narrow, and precipitous channel through which we had passed on our voyage north when we put into the harbor to have the captain's leg set. Negotiating this channel—I should say it was about two miles long—was another illustration of our captain's seamanship. We had to tack innumerable times from one side of the channel to the other, our jib-boom at every tack projecting over the land before the brig came around. We finally dropped anchor opposite the old, cross-crowned Greek church which stands in the center of the struggling village.

16

Slim Goes on Strike

IT was the heart of the Arctic summer and the high hills that rose all about the town were green with deep grass—it looked as if it would reach a man's waist—and ablaze with wild flowers. I was surprised to see such a riot of blooms in this far northern latitude, but there they were, and every off-shore breeze was sweet with their fragrance. The village was dingy enough, but the country looked alluring and, as the day after we dropped anchor was Sunday and nothing to do aboard, the crew decided to ask for a day's liberty ashore. Bill White, the Englishman, and Slim, our Royal Life Guardsman, agreed to act as the forecastle's ambassadors to the cabin. They dressed up in their smartest clothes and went aft to interview Captain Shorey on the quarter-deck. White made the speech of the occasion and proffered the forecastle's request in his best rhetoric.

Captain Shorey puffed silently at his cigar. "I'll see about it," he said. That closed the incident as far as the captain was concerned. We got no shore leave.

As the day wore away and the desired permission failed to materialize, the forecastle became piqued at what it considered the skipper's gratuitous ungraciousness. Slim waxed particularly indignant.

"He'll see about it," Slim sneered. "He never had no idea of letting us go in the first place. He's a cold-blooded son of a sea cook—that's what he is—and as for me, I'll never do another tap of work aboard the bloody hooker."

This was strong language. Of course, none of us took it seriously, feeling sure Slim would reconsider by the next morning and turn to for work with the rest of us. But we did not know Slim. Bright and early Monday morning, the men mustered on deck and went to work, but Slim remained in his bunk.

Having rowed our whale bone to the dock and stored it in a warehouse to await the first steamer for San Francisco, a boat's crew towed three or four hogsheads roped together ashore for water. Another boat went ashore for coal.

Those left aboard the brig were put to work in the hold near the main hatch under the supervision of Mr. Winchester. The mate suddenly noted Slim's absence.

"Where's Slim?" he asked.

Nobody answered.

"He didn't go ashore in the boats," said the mate. "Where is he?"

Someone volunteered that Slim was sick.

"Sick, eh?" said the mate.

He hustled off to the forecastle scuttle.

"Slim," he sang out, "what's the matter with you?"

"I'm sick," responded Slim from his bunk.

"If you're sick," said the mate, "come aft and report yourself sick to the captain."

In a little while, Slim shuffled back to the cabin. A few minutes later wild yells came from the cabin. We stopped work. The mate seemed to think we might rush to the rescue.

"Get busy there," he roared. "Slew that cask around."

The yells broke off. We went to work again. For a half hour, there was silence in the cabin. We wondered what had happened. Slim might have been murdered for all we knew. Finally Slim emerged and went silently forward. We noticed a large shaved spot on the top of his head where two long strips of court-plaster formed a black cross.

The first thing Slim did after getting back to the forecastle was to take one of his blue flannel shirts and, while none of the officers was looking, shin up the ratlines and hang it on the fore-lift. This is an old-time sailor sign of distress and means trouble aboard. The mate soon spied the shirt swinging in the breeze.

"Well, I'll be darned," he said. "Jump up there one of you and take that shirt down."

No one stirred. The mate called the cabin boy and the young Kanaka brought down the shirt. Slim told us at dinner time all about his adventure in the cabin.

"I goes down in the cabin," said Slim, "and the captain is standing with his hands in his pants pockets, smiling friendly-like. 'Hello, Slim,' he says. 'Sit down in this chair.' I sits down and the captain says, 'Well, my boy, what's the matter with you?' 'I'm sick,' says I. 'Where do you feel bad?' he says. 'I ache all over,' says I.

"He steps over in front of me, still with that little smile on his face, 'I've got good medicine aboard this ship,' he says, 'and I'll fix you up in a jiffy, my boy,' says he. With that he jerks one of his hands out of his pocket and he has a revolver clutched in it. 'Here's the medicine you need,' he says and he bats me over the cocoanut with the gun.

"The blood spurts all over me and I jumps up and yells, but the captain points his pistol at me and orders me to sit down again. He storms up and down the cabin floor. 'I'll teach you who's master aboard this ship,' he shouts and for a minute he was so purple in the face with rage, I thought he was going to murder me for sure. By and by he cools down. 'Well, Slim,' he says, 'I guess I hit you a little harder than I meant to, but I'm a bad man when I get started. You need tending to now, sure enough.'

"So he has the cabin boy fetch a pan of warm water and he washes the blood out of my hair with his own hands and then shaves around the cut and pastes sticking plaster on. That's all. But say, will I have the law on him when we get back to Frisco? Will I?"

It was a long way back to Frisco. In the meantime we wondered what was in store for the luckless Irish grenadier. That afternoon, the revenue cutter *Corwin* came steaming into port towing a poaching sealer as a prize. It was the same schooner, we learned, we had seen the *Corwin* chasing a few days before.

As the cutter passed us, Slim sprang on the forecastle head while Captain Shorey and everybody aboard the brig looked at him and, waving a blue flannel shirt frantically, shouted: "Please come aboard. I've had trouble aboard."

"Aye, aye," came back across the water from the government patrol vessel. Waving a shirt has no significance in sea tradition, but Slim was not enough of a sailor to know that, and besides, he wanted to leave nothing undone to impress the revenue cutter officers with the urgency of his case.

No sooner had the *Corwin* settled to her berth at the pier than a small boat with bluejackets at the oars, two officers in gold braid and epaulettes in the stern, and with the stars and stripes flying, shot out from under her quarter and headed for the brig.

"Aha," we chuckled. "Captain Shorey has got his foot in it. He has Uncle Sam to deal with now. He won't hit him over the head with a revolver."

The boat came alongside and the officers climbed over the rail. Captain Shorey welcomed them with a smile and elaborate courtesy and ushered them into the cabin. Slim was sent for.

"Tell 'em everything, Slim," we urged. "Give it to the captain hot and heavy. He's a brute and the revenue cutter men will take you off the brig as sure as shooting. They won't dare leave you aboard to lead a dog's life for the rest of the voyage."

"I'll show him up, all right," was Slim's parting shot.

Slim came back from the cabin a little later.

"I told 'em everything," he said. "They listened to everything I had to say and took down a lot of notes in a book. I asked 'em to take me off the brig right away, for, says I, Captain Shorey will kill me if they leave me aboard. I guess they'll take me off."

An hour later, the two officers of the *Corwin* emerged from the cabin, accompanied by Captain Shorey. They were puffing complacently at a couple of the captain's cigars. They seemed in high good humor. After shaking hands with Captain Shorey, they climbed down into their boat and were rowed back to their vessel. That was the last we ever saw of them. Poor Slim was left to his fate.

And his fate was a rough one. There was no outward change in the attitude of the captain or the officers of the brig toward him. Whenever they spoke to him, they did it with as much civility as they showed the rest of us. But Slim was compelled to work on deck all day and stand his regular night watches into the bargain. That meant he got eight hours sleep during twenty-four hours one day and four hours sleep during the next. As the ship was in whaling waters from now on, the crew had little to do except man the boats. But Slim always had plenty to do. While we smoked our pipes and lounged about, he was kept washing paint work, slushing down masts, scraping deck and knocking the rust off the anchors. Any one of a hundred and one little jobs that didn't need doing, Slim did. This continued until the brig squared her yards for the homeward voyage. Slim had more than three months of it. The Lord knows it was enough. When his nagging finally ended, he was a pale, haggard shadow of his former self. It almost killed him.

17

Into the Arctic

FROM Unalaska, we headed north for the Arctic Ocean. For one day of calm, we lay again off the little Eskimo village of St. Lawrence Bay and again had the natives as our guests. Peter made an elaborate toilet in expectation of seeing once more his little Eskimo sweetheart, but she did not come aboard. A little breeze came walking over the sea and pushed us on northward. On August 15, we sailed through Bering Straits and were at last in the Arctic.

The straits are thirty-six miles wide, with East Cape, a rounded, dome-shaped mass of black basalt, on the Asiatic side and on the American side Cape Prince of Wales, a headland of sharper outline, but neither so lofty nor so sheer. In between the two capes and in line with them, lie the two islands of Big and Little Diomede.

Through the three narrow channels between the capes and the islands, the tide runs with the swiftness of a river's current.

The Eskimos constantly cross from continent to continent in small boats. In still weather the passage can be made in a light kayak with perfect safety. The widest of the three channels is that between Big Diomede and East Cape and is, I should say, not more than fifteen miles across. While we were passing through the straits, we saw a party of Eskimos in a skin boat paddling leisurely across from America to Asia. They no doubt had been on a visit to relatives or friends on the neighboring continent. We were told that in winter when the straits are frozen solidly, the Eskimos frequently walk from one continent to the other.

While we were sailing close to the American shore soon after passing through the straits, the cry of "Walrus, walrus!" from the mast-head sent the crew hurrying to the rail to catch a glimpse of these strange creatures which we had not before encountered. We were passing an immense herd. The shore was crowded with giant bulks, lying perfectly still in the sun, while the waters close to land were alive with bobbing heads. At a distance and at first glance, those on shore looked like a vast herd of cattle resting after grazing. They were as big as oxen and when the sun had dried them, they were of a pronounced reddish color. Those in the water looked black.

They had a way of sticking their heads and necks straight up out of the sea which was slightly suggestive of men treading water. Their heads seemed small for their great bodies and with their big eyes, their beard-like mass of thick bristles about the nose, and their long ivory tusks they had a distinctly human look despite their grotesque ugliness. They lifted their multitudinous voices in gruff, barking roars like so many bulldogs affected with a cold. There must have been 10,000 of them. They paid little attention to the ship. Those on shore remained as motionless as boulders.

"Want to collect a little ivory?" Captain Shorey said with a smile to Mr. Winchester.

"No, thank you, not just now," replied the mate. "I want to live to get back to Frisco."

An ivory hunter among those tusked thousands doubtless would have fared disastrously. Walrus are famous fighters. When attacked, they sometimes upset a boat with their tusks and drown the hunters. They are dangerous even in small herds. Moreover they are difficult to kill. Their thick hides will turn a bullet that does not hit them solidly. Though slow and unwieldy on land or ice, they are surprisingly agile in the water and a harpooned walrus will frequently tow a boat at a dizzy clip.

The region about Cape Prince of Wales is a favorite feeding ground for the animals. The coasts swarm with clams, mussels, and other shell-fish upon which the walrus live. Thirteen varieties of edible clams, it is said, have been discovered by scientists about Cape Prince of Wales. The walrus dig these shell-fish out of the sand and rocks with their tusks, crush them with their teeth, eject the shells, and swallow the dainty tidbits. Their tusks serve them also as weapons of defense and as hooks by which to haul themselves upon ice floes.

We did not dare take chances in the boats among such vast numbers of these formidable creatures and soon left the great herd astern. A little higher up the coast we ran into a small herd numbering about a hundred, and Mr. Winchester, armed with his repeating rifle, lowered his boat to have a try for ivory.

When the mate's boat dashed among the animals they did not dive or run away, but held their ground, standing well up out of water and coughing out defiance. Long John darted a harpoon into one of the beasts and it plunged below and went scurrying away. One might have thought the boat was fast to a young whale from the way the line sizzled out over the bow. The walrus dragged the boat about half a mile, and when the animal again came to the surface for air Mr. Winchester killed it with a bullet.

But the blood and the shooting had thrown the remainder of the herd into violent excitement. Roaring furiously, the great beasts converged from all sides in the wake of the chase. By the time Long John had cut off the head of the dead walrus and heaved it aboard and had recovered his harpoon, the animals were swarming menacingly about the boat. Long John, who had been in such ticklish situations before, began to beat a tattoo on the gunwales with his sheath knife, at the same time emitting a series of blood-curdling yells. This was intended to awe the boat's besiegers and had a momentary effect. The brutes stood in the water apparently puzzled, but still roaring savagely. But they were not long to be held off by mere noise. Led by a monster bull, they rushed at the boat in a concerted attack. The sailors belabored them over the head with the sweeps. The mate pumped lead into them from his rifle. Still they came on. When Captain

Shorey, who had been watching the battle from the quarter-deck, saw how serious the situation was becoming, he grew alarmed.

"Those men will be killed," he shouted to Mr. Landers. "Call the watch and lower those other boats, and be quick about it."

In a jiffy the boats were lowered, the crews piled in, masts were stepped, and we shot away to the rescue. But the mate's crew solved their own problem before we could come into action. When it seemed likely the walrus would swamp the boat, Long John harpooned the leader of the herd. The big walrus dived and made off, hauling the boat out of the midst of the furious brutes to safety. The other animals did not pursue. They bobbed about the scene of the conflict for some time and finally disappeared. Long John killed the big bull to which the boat was fast, cut off its head, and the boat went back to the battleground to take similar toll of the walrus that had died under the mate's rain of bullets. Eight carcasses were found afloat and as many more probably had sunk.

Ten heads with their ivory tusks were brought aboard the brig as trophies of the hunt. The tusks of the bull that had led the attack measured two feet six inches. The animal, according to Mr. Winchester, must have been ten or twelve feet long. The mate estimated its weight at 1,800 pounds—a guess, of course, but perhaps a close one.

18

Blubber and Song

W E were cruising in open water soon afterward with two whaling ships in sight, the *Reindeer* and the *Helen Marr*, both barkentines and carrying five boats each, when we raised a school of bowheads straight ahead and about five miles distant. There were twenty-five or thirty whales and a broad patch of sea was covered with their incessant fountains.

The other ships saw them about the same time. The long-drawn, musical "Blo-o-o-w!" from their mastheads came to us across the water.

Aboard the brig, the watch was called and all hands were mustered to the boats. Falls were thrown off the hooks and we stood by to lower as soon as the captain gave the word. There was equal bustle on the other ships. Traveling before a favoring breeze in the same direction as the whales, the three vessels waited until they could work closer. Each captain in the meanwhile kept a watchful eye on the others. None of them proposed to let his rivals get the start. The *Reindeer* was to windward of us, the *Helen Marr* on our lee.

When the ships had reached within a mile of the whales Captain Shorey sent our boats down. Instantly the other skippers did the same. Soon thirteen whale boats were speeding on the chase.

Fine sailing weather it was, with a fresh breeze ruffling the surface of a gently heaving sea. With all sails set and keeping well apart, the boats heeled over, their crews sitting lined up along the weather gunwales. There seemed no chance of any clash or misunderstanding. There were plenty of whales, and with any luck there would be glory enough and profit enough for all.

Like a line of skirmishers deployed against an enemy, the boats stole silently toward the whales. We soon saw the great animals were busy feeding. A few inches below the surface the sea was filled with "whale food," a round, diaphanous, disk-like jellyfish about the size of a silver dollar and perfectly white. When we arrived in this Arctic Ocean whale pasture the water seemed snowy with the millions of jellyfish. With open jaws, the whales swam this way and that, making zigzag swaths a hundred yards long through the gelatinous masses, their great heads and backs well out of water, their fins now and then flapping ponderously. When they had entangled a sufficient quantity of the jellyfish in the long hair hanging from the inner edges of their teeth they closed their mouths with reverberating snaps that sent the water splashing out on either side.

Before the whales were aware of danger, the boats rushed in among them. Each boatheader singled out a whale, and five boats were quickly fast—two from the *Reindeer*, two from the *Helen Marr*, and Mr. Winchester's boat. Wild turmoil and confusion instantly ensued among the great animals. They went plunging below in alarm and the boats that made no strike at the first onslaught had no chance thereafter. The whales did not stop to investigate the causes of the sudden interruption of their banquet. The sea swallowed them up and we did not see them again. A little later we caught a glimpse of their fountains twinkling against the sky on the far horizon.

Mr. Winchester's whale was wriggling about among the jellyfish with jaws widely distended when the boat slipped silently upon it. As the prow bumped against its black skin, Long John drove a harpoon up to the hitches in its back.

With a tonite bomb shattered in its vitals, the monster sounded in a smother of foam. In the dynamic violence with which it got under way it literally stood on its head. Its flukes, easily twenty feet from tip to tip, shot at least thirty feet into the air. They swung over to one side, the great body forming a high arch, and struck the sea with a resounding smack. Then they sailed on high again to come down on the other side with another broadside smash. Again they rose like lightning into the air and the whale seemed to slip down perpendicularly into the ocean.

It was evident at the outset that the animal was badly wounded. It swam only a short distance below the surface and not rapidly, sending up thousands of bubbles to mark its course. This broad highway of bubbles curved and turned, but Mr. Winchester, who had been smart enough not to lower his sail, followed it as a hound follows the trail of a deer. The boat sailed almost as swiftly as the whale swam and was able to keep almost directly above it. When the whale came to the surface the mate was upon it and Long John's second harpoon stopped it dead in its track. The whale went through no flurry, but died instantly and rolled over on its back.

With excitement all about, there was nothing for Mr. Landers or Gabriel to do. So we sat still in the boats and watched the swift incidents of the far-flung battle.

One of the whales struck by a boat from the *Reindeer* breached almost completely out of water as soon as it felt the sting of the harpoon. It floundered down like a falling tower, rolled about for a moment before sinking to a swimming depth, and made off at mad speed. It rose within twenty feet of where our boat lay at a stand still and we could see its wild eye, as big as a saucer, as the injured creature blew up a fountain whose bloody spray fell all over us. The boat it was dragging soon went flashing past us, the crew sitting crouched down and silent.

"Swing to him, fellers," shouted Kaiuli, standing up and waving his hat about his head.

But the others paid no attention to our South Sea island savage. They were intent just then on tragedy. Their boat struck the whale at its next rise. The animal went into a violent flurry. It beat the sea into a lather with fins and flukes and darted around on its side in a semicircle, clashing its great jaws, until it finally collapsed and lay limp and lifeless.

The whale struck by the other boat from the *Reindeer* ran out a tub of line, but a second boat had come up in time to bend on its own line and took the animal in tow. Before the whale had run out this new tub, a third boat harpooned it. With two boats fast to it, it continued its flight to windward and was at least two miles from us when its pursuers at last overtook and killed it.

Two boats from the *Helen Marr* struck whales while the monsters were feeding within an oar's length of each other. One whale started off at right angles to the direction taken by the other. It looked for a time as if the two lines would become entangled and the boats would crash together. But the whale that cut across the other's course swam above the latter's line and dragged its boat so swiftly after it that a collision was averted by a few feet.

One of the whales was bombed and killed after a short flight. The other acted in a way that whales hardly ever act. It ran hard to windward at first, as whales usually do when struck. Then it suddenly turned and ran in an exactly opposite direction. This unexpected change in its course almost upset the boat, which was jerked violently over on its beam-ends and spun round like a top, while the crew held on for dear life and barely escaped being pitched in to the sea. Once righted and on its way again, the boat rapidly hauled up on the whale, whose fast-going vitality showed in its diminished speed. After a flight that had covered at least a mile, the whale was finally killed close to the spot at which it had first been struck.

When the sharp, fast work of the boats ended, five mighty carcasses lay stretched upon the sea. The great whale drive, which had lasted less than an hour, had bagged game worth something like $60,000.

The three ships soon sailed to close quarters and the boats had a comparatively easy time getting the whales alongside. That night the try-works were started and big cressets whose flames were fed by "scrap" flared up on all the ships, lighting them in ghostly-wise from the deck to the topmost sail.

At the cutting in of this whale I had my first experience at the windlass. The heaviest labor falls to the sailors who man the windlass and hoist in the great blanket pieces of blubber and the "old head." Gabriel, the happiest-spirited old soul aboard, bossed the job, as he always did, and cheered the sailors and made the hard work seem like play by his constant chanteys—those catchy, tuneful, working songs of the sea. All the old sailors on the brig knew these songs by heart and often sang them on the topsail halyard or while reefing on the topsail yard. The green hands soon picked up the words and airs of the choruses and joined in. The day laborer on land has no idea how work at sea is lightened by these songs.

Gabriel knew no end of them, and in a round, musical voice led the men at the windlass in such rollicking old-time sea airs as "Whiskey for the Johnnies," "Blow the Man Down," "Blow, Boys, Blow," and "Rolling Rio." He would sing a verse and the sailors would stand with their hands on the windlass bars until he had concluded. Then they would heave away with a will and make the pawls clank and clatter as they roared out the chorus.

The old Negro's favorite was "Whiskey for the Johnnies." It had a fine rousing chorus and we liked to sing it not only for its stirring melody but because we always harbored a hope—which, I may add, was never realized—that the captain would be touched by the words and send forward a drop of liquor with which to wet our whistles. Gabriel would begin in this way:

"O whiskey is the life of man."

And the sailors as they heaved would chorus:

"O whiskey, O Johnny.
O whiskey is the life of man,
Whiskey for the Johnnies."

Then Gabriel would sing:

> "Whiskey killed my poor old dad,
> Whiskey drove my mother mad,
> Whiskey caused me much abuse,
> Whiskey put me in the calaboose,
> Whiskey fills a man with care,
> Whiskey makes a man a bear."

And the men would come through with the refrain:

> "O Whiskey, O Johnny.
> I drink whiskey when I can.
> O whiskey for the Johnnies."

At the end of our song which ran through verses enough to bring a blanket piece of blubber swinging inboard, we would look wistfully toward the quarter-deck and wonder if the "old man" would take our musical hint.

Or Gabriel would start up "Rolling Rio":

> "I'll sing you a song of the fish of the sea."

The men would thunder:

> "Rolling Rio."

Gabriel would continue:

> "As I was going down Broadway Street
> A pretty young girl I chanced to meet."

And the sailors would sing:

> "To my rolling Rio Grande.
> Hurrah, you Rio, rolling Rio.
> So fare you well, my pretty young girl,
> I'm bound for the Rio Grande."

"Blow, Boys, Blow" was another with which we made the Arctic ring. The other ships could not have failed to hear its swinging rhythm as it burst from our lusty lungs in this fashion:

Gabriel:

> "A Yankee ship came down the river."

The sailors:

> "Blow, boys, blow."

Gabriel:

> "And who do you think was skipper of her?
> Dandy Jim of old Carolina."

Sailors:

> "Blow, my bully boys, blow."

Gabriel:

> "And who do you think was second greaser?
> Why, Pompey Squash, that big buck nigger."

Sailors:

> "Blow, boys, blow."

Gabriel:

> "And what do you think they had for dinner?
> Monkey lights and donkey's liver."

Sailors:

> "Blow, my bully boys, blow."

Gabriel:

> "And what do you think they had for supper?
> Old hardtack and Yankee leather.
> Then blow, my boys, for better weather.
> Blow, my boys, I love to hear you."

Sailors:

"Blow, my bully boys, blow."

So with a heave and a song we soon had our whale stowed, bone and blubber, below hatches. The *Reindeer* and the *Helen Marr* had drifted far away from us by the time our work was finished, but they were still in sight and their try-works smoking. Our whale yielded 1,800 pounds of bone.

19

A Narrow Pinch

THE whaling fleet divided soon after entering the Arctic Ocean. Some of the ships went straight on north to the whaling grounds about Point Barrow and Herschel Island. The others bore to the westward for the whaling along the ice north of eastern Siberia. We stood to the westward. In a few days we had raised the white coasts of a continent of ice that shut in all the north as far as the eye could see and extended to the Pole and far beyond. With the winds in the autumn always blowing from the northwest, the sea was perfectly calm in the lee of this indestructible polar cap. I have been out in the whale boats when they were heeled over on their beam-ends under double-reefed sails before a gale of wind upon a sea as smooth as the waters of a duck pond. It was now no longer bright twilight at midnight. The sun already well on its journey to the equator, sank earlier and deeper below the horizon. Several hours of darkness began to intervene between its setting and its rising. By September we had a regular succession of days and nights.

With the return of night we saw for the first time that electric phenomenon of the Far North, the aurora borealis. Every night during our stay in the Arctic the skies were made brilliant with these shooting lights. I had expected to see waving curtains of rainbow colors, but I saw no colors at any time. The auroras of those skies were of pure white light. A great arch would suddenly shoot across the zenith from horizon to horizon. It was nebulously bright, like a shining milky way or a path of snow upon which moonlight sparkles. You could hear it rustle and crackle distinctly, with a sound like that of heavy silk violently shaken. It shed a cold white radiance over the sea like the light of arc lamps, much brighter than the strongest moonlight.

It was not quite bright enough to read by— but almost—and it threw sharp, black shadows on the deck. Gradually the arch would fade, to be succeeded by others that spanned the heavens from other angles. Often several arches and segments were in the sky at the same time.

Sometimes, though rarely, the aurora assumed the form of a curtain hanging vertically along the horizon and shimmered as though agitated by a strong wind.

I was pleasantly surprised by the temperatures encountered in the Arctic. We were in the polar ocean until early in October, but the lowest temperature recorded by the brig's thermometer was 10 degrees below zero. Such a temperature seems colder on sea than on land. Greater dampness has something to do with it, but imagination probably plays its part. There is something in the very look of a winter sea, yeasty under the north wind and filled with snowy floes and icebergs, that seems to congeal the marrow in one's bones. In the cold snaps, when a big wave curled over the bows, I have seen it break and strike upon the deck in the form of hundreds of ice pellets. Almost every day when it was rough, the old Arctic played marbles with us.

What with the mists, the cold rains, the sleets and snows and flying spray, the brig was soon a mass of ice. The sides became encased in a white armor of ice which at the bows was several feet thick. We frequently had to knock it off. The decks were sheeted with ice, the masts and spars were glazed with it, the shrouds, stays, and every rope were coated with ice, and the yard-arms and foot-ropes were hung with ice stalactites. One of the most beautiful sights I ever saw was the whaling fleet when we fell in with it one cold, gray morning. The frost had laid its white witchery upon the other ships as it had upon the brig, and they glided through the black seas, pallid, shimmering, and phantomlike in their ice armor—an armada of ghostly *Flying Dutchmen.*

The brig was constantly wearing and tacking on the whaling grounds and there was considerable work to be done aloft. By the captain's orders, we did such work with our mittens off. Hauling bare-handed on ropes of solid ice was painful labor, and "Belay all!" often came like a benediction to souls in torment. Then we had much ado whipping our hands against our sides to restore the circulation. After Big Foot Louis had frozen a finger, the captain permitted us to keep our mittens on.

Work aloft under such conditions was dangerous. Our walrus-hide boots were heelless and extremely slippery and our footing on the foot-ropes was precarious. We had to depend as much upon our hands as upon our feet to keep from falling when strung out for reefing along the topsail yard. Many were the slips and hair-breadth escapes. It seems now, on looking back on it, almost miraculous that some of us green hands did not tumble to our death.

We saw whales frequently. Sometimes the boats were lowered half a dozen times a day. Often we spent whole days in the boats, and even in our skin clothes it was freezing business sitting still on the gunwale of a beam-ended boat driving along at thrilling speed in the teeth of an Arctic gale. Our skipper was a good gambler, and he lowered whenever there was an off chance to bag a leviathan.

As we worked to the westward, twin peaks rose out of the sea ahead of us. Covered with snow and ice, they stood out against the sky as white as marble. It was our first glimpse of Herald Island, in latitude 71 degrees North. We sailed north of the island and close to it. It looked forbiddingly desolate. Along the shores there was a rampart of black rock. Nowhere else was a glimpse of earth or herbage of any sort. The island was a gleaming white mass of snow and ice from the dark sea to the tips of the twin mountains. It was discovered in 1849 by Captain Kellett of the English ship *Herald* and named after his vessel. Captain De Long, leader of the ill-fated *Jeanette* expedition, was frozen in close to the island in the winter of 1880. He found polar bear plentiful and trapped and shot a number.

Here at Herald Island we fell in with eighteen ships of the whaling fleet—all that had cruised to the westward—and it was only by good luck that some of them did not leave their hulks on those desolate shores. The polar pack rested solidly against the island's western end and curved in a great half-moon to the north and east. The pocket thus formed between the island and the ice looked good for whales and the ships hunted it out carefully.

Far to the eastward, a long arm of ice reached out from the pack and grasped the island's eastern end. This arm was perhaps a mile wide. It barred our passage back to the open sea. The ships had been caught in a trap. They were bottled up in a hole of water perhaps a hundred square miles in extent. Busy on the lookout for whales, the captains of the fleet did not realize the situation for several hours. When they discovered their predicament, they hurried to the crow's-nests with glasses to try to spy out an avenue of escape. Sail was cracked on. The ships began to fly about like panic-stricken living creatures.

The great polar pack was pressing rapidly toward the island. Unless the ships escaped, it seemed likely they would be securely hemmed in before night. In this event, if they escaped wreck by ice pressure they faced the prospect of lying still in an ice bed until the pack broke up in the spring.

All day long the frightened ships scurried up and down the ice barrier without finding an opening. They ran to the westward. There was no escape there. They flew back to the east. An ice wall confronted them. The case seemed hopeless. The panic of the captains became more and more evident. If a ship hurried off in any direction, the other ships flocked after her like so many scared sheep. Morning and afternoon passed in this wild search for an outlet. Night was coming on.

A bark squared her yards and shot away to the southeast. It was the *Sea Breeze*. When the others expected her to tack, she did no such thing, but kept going straight ahead. On she went alone, far from the fleet. It was exciting to watch that single ship flying eastward. What could it mean? Had she found an opening? The other ships turned their prows after her, one by one. A long line of vessels soon was careering in the wake of the *Sea Breeze*. She had dwindled to a little ship in the far distance when at last we saw her break out the American colors at her mizzen peak. Every man aboard the brig gave a cheer. Cheers from the other ships came across the water. It meant that the *Sea Breeze* was clear.

She had found a lead that suddenly had opened through the eastern ice strip, as leads will open in drifting floes. The lead was not entirely clear. A narrow strip of ice lay across it. The *Sea Breeze* butted through this strip and sailed on to freedom. The other vessels followed. Our brig was the tenth ship to pass through. As we negotiated the narrow passage, the ice was so close on both sides we could have leaped upon it from the bulwarks. It was with a joyous sense of escape that we cleared the pack and swung once more on the open sea. Soon after the last ship of the fleet had bumped her way to safety the ice closed solidly behind.

20

A Race and a Race Horse

E ARLY one morning the old familiar cry rang
from the crow's-nest—"Blo-o-o-w." A lone
whale, in plain view from the deck, was sporting
lazily on the surface about a mile and a half off our
starboard bow. The three boats were hurriedly
lowered and the crews scrambled in. We took to the
oars, for not a breath of air was stirring and the sea
was as smooth as polished silver. Away went the boats
together, as if from a starting line at the crack of a
pistol, with the whale as the goal and prize of the race.

Mr. Winchester had often boasted of the
superiority of his crew. Mr. Landers had not
seemed interested in the question, but Gabriel
resented the assumption.

"Just wait," he used to say to us confiden-
tially. "Well show him which is de bes' crew.
Our time'll come."

The men of the mate's boat had shared their officer's vainglorious opinion. They had long swaggered among us with a self-complacent assurance that made us smart. Our chance had at last come to prove their pride a mockery under the skipper's eyes. If ever men wanted, from the bottom of their hearts, to win, we did. We not only had our name as skillful oarsmen to vindicate, but a grudge to wipe out.

So evenly matched were the crews that the boats rushed along side by side for at least half a mile, Mr. Winchester insouciant and superciliously smiling, Mr. Landers indifferent, Gabriel all eagerness and excitement. Perhaps Mr. Landers knew his crew was outclassed. If he did not, he was not long in finding it out, for his boat began to drop steadily behind and was soon hopelessly out of the contest. But the other two crews, stroke for stroke, were proving foemen worthy of each other's prowess.

"Oho, Gabriel," Mr. Winchester laughed contemptuously, "you think your boat can out-pull us, eh? Bet you ten pounds of tobacco we beat you to the whale."

"I take you," cried Gabriel excitedly. "Dat's a bet."

If Gabriel accepted the challenge, so did we, and right heartily at that. We threw ourselves, heart and soul, into the struggle. The men in the mate's boat, holding us cheaply, believed they could draw away whenever they chose and go on to win, hands down. The mate kept looking over at us, a supercilious smile still curling the corners of his mouth.

"Come on now, my boys," he cried. "All together. Shake her up a bit. Give those fellows a taste of your mettle."

We heard his words as distinctly as his own crew heard them—he was only a few boat lengths away. They inspired us to greater exertion than they inspired his own men. They spurted. So did we. Still the two boats raced neck and neck. We were not to be shaken off. The mate looked disconcerted. His men had done their level best to take the lead and they had failed. That spurt marked the crisis of the race.

The mate's smile faded out. His face grew anxious. Then it hardened into an expression of grim determination. He had sat motionless at the beginning. Now when he saw his vaunted superiority slipping through his fingers he began to "jockey"—throwing his body forward in violent lunges at every stroke of the sweeps, pushing with all his might on the stroke oar, and booming out, "Pull, my boys; pull away, my boys."

But old Gabriel was "jockeying," too, and encouraging us in the same fashion.

"We show dat mate," he kept repeating. "We show him. Steady together, my lads. Pull away!"

And we pulled as if our lives depended on it, bending to the oars with every ounce of our strength, making the long sweeps bend in the water. We began to forge ahead, very slowly, inch by inch. We saw it—it cheered us to stronger effort. Our rivals saw it—it discouraged them. Under the heart-breaking strain they began to tire. They slipped back little by little. They spurted again. It was no use. We increased our advantage. Open daylight began to broaden between the stern of our boat and the bow of theirs. They were beaten in a fair trial of strength, oarsmanship, and endurance.

"Ha, my boys," chuckled Gabriel. "We win. Good-by to dat mate. Now we catch dat whale."

We shot along at undiminished speed, pulling exultantly. What the whale was doing or how close we were to it, we at the oars could not see.

"Stand by, Louis," said Gabriel presently.

"Aye, aye, sir," responded Louis.

A few more strokes and a great black bulk loomed close alongside.

"Give it to him, Louis," cried Gabriel.

And as the boat glanced against that island of living ebony, Louis's harpoon sank deep into the soft, buttery mass. We heard the tiny concussion of the cap of the tonite gun, and a fraction of a second later the bomb exploded with a muffled roar in the whale's vitals.

"Stern, stern!" shouted Gabriel. "Stern for your lives!"

We backed water as hard as we could. The great back went flashing down, the mighty tail rose up directly over us, shutting out the sky. It curled over away from us and smote the sea with deafening thunder. As quick as lightning it rose into the air again, curled high above us with tragic menace, and came crashing down, this time toward us. But we had backed just out of harm's way. Death and that terrible tail missed us by about three feet.

The mate's boat came rushing up. It was too late. The whale—our whale—had sounded.

"Your boat can beat us, eh?" Gabriel called tauntingly to Mr. Winchester. "Not much. I know we break black skin first. I know we win dat race."

Our line began to dance and sing, leaping up from its neatly laid coils in the tub in dizzy spirals and humming out over the bow.

"Ha, boys," sang out Kaiuli, our Kanaka bow oarsman. "Now for fine ride behind Arctic race horse—eh?"

With a whale harnessed to our boat and a sea as smooth as any turnpike for our highway, we settled ourselves for the ride. The friction of the line set the boat going. It gathered momentum. In a little while we were tearing along through that sea of oil, our bow deep in the smother as the whale pulled down upon it, and flashing walls of white spray flaring out on either side.

The other boats pulled for the point at which it seemed most probable the whale would come up. When it rose to the surface, the mate's boat was nearest.

"Lay me on four seas off and I'll get him," we heard Long John shout to Mr. Winchester.

The mate did just that. The whale was up but a moment and Long John tried for it, but it was too long a dart, and his harpoon fell into the sea. Before he had recovered his iron we had shot past. When the whale rose again, we bumped out of water on its body. A second harpoon drove home in its back, a second bomb exploded in its insides. A great shudder seized the monster. The water foamed white with its throes. Then everything grew still. Slowly the great body rolled over, belly up.

Big Foot Louis danced up and down in the bow, raising his knees high in a sort of joyful cake-walk. Gabriel, equally excited, waved his hat.

"By golly," he shouted, "dat mate don't strike him. Dat feesh is all ours. It takes old Gabriel fer kill de whale, by golly."

When we got back to the brig we looked like snow-powdered Santa Clauses. The spray kicked up in our wild ride behind the Arctic Ocean race horse had wet us from head to foot and, freezing on our fur clothes, had frosted us all over with fine white ice. Mr. Winchester was a good sportsman and paid his bet promptly. Out of his winnings Gabriel gave each man of his boat's crew a plug of tobacco.

After the whale had been brought alongside the ship and the blubber had been peeled off its body, it fell to the lot of Big Foot Louis to cut in the "old head." It was his first opportunity to show his experience in such work and he was as elated as a boy. He threw off his coat with a theatrical flourish, hitched up his trousers, seized an axe, and with an air of bravado climbed down on the stripped carcass. A little sea had begun to run and the whale was bending sinuously throughout its length and rolling slightly from side to side.

Louis chopped two little ledges in the whale's flesh with the deftness of an old hand, and planting his feet in these, began raining blows with his axe on the neck. He was getting on famously, and the crew, hanging over the bulwarks, was watching with admiring eyes. Suddenly the whale gave an unexpectedly violent roll—our Arctic Ocean race horse was proving a bronco even in death—and Louis's big foot slipped off into the water. He lost his balance, pitched forward, and sprawled face downward on the whale, his axe sailing away and plunking into the sea. He clutched frantically at the whale, but every grip slipped loose and, inch by inch, with eyeballs popping out of his head, he slid off into the sea and with a yell went under.

Everybody laughed. The captain held his sides and the officers on the cutting stage almost fell off in the violence of their mirth. Louis came up spluttering and splashing. He was an expert swimmer, as expert as the Kanakas among whom he had lived for years, and he needed all his skill to keep afloat in his heavy boots and skin clothes.

As soon as the mate could control his merriment, he stuck the long handle of his spade down and Louis grasped it and was pulled back on the whale's body. He sat there, dripping and shivering and with chattering teeth, rolling his white eyes up at the laughing crew along the rail with a tragic "Et tu, Brute" expression. He couldn't see the joke.

"Lemme aboard," he whimpered.

"Stay where you are," roared the captain, "and cut in that head."

Louis lived in mortal fear of the skipper, and the way he straightened up in his slippery seat and said "Aye, aye, sir!" made the crew burst out laughing again. Another axe was passed down to him. He floundered to his feet, and though he found it harder than ever in his wet boots to keep his footing, and slipped more than once and almost fell off again, he finally succeeded in cutting off the head. He had regained his air of bravado by the time he had scrambled back on deck.

"Pretty close shave, Louis," ventured a sailor.

"Humph," returned Louis, "dat's nothin'—nothin' at all." And with quite lordly dignity, despite the dripping brine, he stalked off to the cabin to change his clothes.

21

Bears for a Change

SOON after taking our third whale, we saw our first polar bears—two of them on a narrow floe of ice. When the brig was within fifty yards of them the mate got out his rifle and began blazing away. His first shot struck one of the bears in the hind leg. The animal wheeled and snapped at the wound. The second shot stretched it out dead. The second bear was hit somewhere in the body and, plunging into the sea, it struck out on a three-mile swim for the main ice pack. It swam with head and shoulders out, cleaving the water like a high-power launch and leaving a creaming wake behind. Moving so swiftly across the brig's course, it made a difficult target.

"I'm going down after that fellow," said Mr. Winchester.

He called a boat's crew and lowered, taking his place in the bow with his rifle, while Long John sat at the tiller. He had got only a short distance from the ship when Captain Shorey ordered Gabriel after him.

"Killing that bear may be a bigger job than he thinks," he said. "Lower a boat, Mr. Gabriel, and lend a hand. It may be needed."

In a few minutes Gabriel was heading after the mate's boat. Neither boat hoisted sail. With four men at the sweeps, it was as much as the boats could do to gain on the brute. If the bear was not making fifteen miles an hour, I'm no judge.

Mr. Winchester kept pegging away, his bullets knocking up water all around the animal. One ball struck the bear in the back. That decided the animal to change its tactics. It quit running away and turned and made directly for its enemies.

"Avast rowing," sang out the mate.

The men peaked their oars, turned on the thwarts, and had their first chance to watch developments, which came thick and fast. Rabid ferocity, blind fury, and deadly menace were in every line of that big white head shooting across the water toward them. The boat sat stationary on a dancing sea. The mate's rifle cracked repeatedly. The bullets peppered the sea, sending up little spurts of water all about the bear. But the beast did not notice them, never tried to dodge, never swerved aside—just kept rushing for the boat with the directness of an arrow.

It was a time of keen excitement for the men in the boat. They kept glancing with an "Oh, that Blücher or night would come" expression toward Gabriel's boat, which was doing all that oars could do to get into the fray, Big Foot Louis standing all the while in the bow with harpoon ready. The bobbing of his boat disconcerted the mate's aim. Though he was a crack shot, as he had often proved among the okchugs, I never saw him shoot so badly. But he kept banging away, and when the bear was within fifteen or twenty yards he got home a ball in its shoulder. The beast plunged into the air, snarling and clawing at the sea, then rushed again for the boat like a white streak. It rammed into the boat bows-on, stuck one mighty paw over the gunwale, and with a snarling roar and a frothing snap of glistening fangs, leaped up and tried to climb aboard.

Just at this critical instant Gabriel's boat came into action with a port helm. Louis drove a harpoon into the beast behind the shoulder—drove it up to the haft, so that the spear-head burst out on the other side. At the same moment the mate stuck the muzzle of his rifle almost down the bear's throat and fired. The great brute fell back into the water, clawed and plunged and roared and clashed its teeth and so, in a whirlwind of impotent fury, died.

For a moment it lay limp and still among the lapping waves, then slowly began to sink. But Louis held it up with the harpoon line and the animal was towed back to the brig. It measured over seven feet in length and weighed 1,700 pounds—a powerful, gaunt old giant, every inch bone and sinew. Mr. Winchester retrieved the other bear from the ice floe. It was considerably smaller. The pelts were stripped off and the carcasses thrown overboard. The skins were in good condition, despite the earliness of the season. They were stretched on frames fashioned by the cooper, and tanned.

A week or so later we sighted a lone bear on an ice floe making a meal off a seal it had killed. It was late in the afternoon and one had to look twice before being able to make out its white body against the background of snow-covered ice. When the brig sailed within seventy-five yards the bear raised its head for a moment, took a squint at the vessel, didn't seem interested, and went on eating.

Resting his rifle on the bulwarks and taking careful aim, Mr. Winchester opened fire. The pattering of the bullets on the ice seemed to puzzle the bear. As it heard the missiles sing and saw the snow spurt up, it left the seal and began walking all about the floe on an investigation. Finally it reared on its hind legs to its full height. While in this upright position, a bullet struck it and turned it a sudden twisting somersault. Its placid mood was instantly succeeded by one of ferocious anger. It looked toward the vessel and roared savagely. Still the bullets fell about it, and now alive to its danger, it plunged into the sea and struck out for the polar pack a mile distant.

Mr. Winchester again lowered, with Gabriel's boat to back him up. The chase was short and swift. The boats began to overhaul the bear as it approached the ice, the mate's bullets splashing all about the animal, but doing no damage. As the brute was hauling itself upon the ice, a ball crashed into its back, breaking its spine. It fell back into the water and expired in a furious flurry. A running bowline having been slipped over its neck, it was towed back to the brig.

Not long afterward, while we were cruising in open water, a polar bear swam across the brig's stern. There was neither ice nor land in sight. Figuring the ship's deck as the center of a circle of vision about ten miles in diameter, the bear already had swum five miles, and probably quite a bit more, and it is certain he had an equal distance to go before finding any ice on which to rest. It probably had drifted south on an ice pan and was bound back for its home on the polar pack.

The bear made too tempting a target for the mate to resist, and he brought out his rifle and, kneeling on the quarter-deck, he took steady aim and fired. His bullet struck about two feet behind the animal. He aimed again, but changed his mind and lowered his gun.

"No," he said, "that fellow's making too fine a swim. I'll let him go."

Cleaving the water with a powerful stroke, the bear went streaking out of sight over the horizon. It is safe to say that before its swim ended the animal covered fifteen miles at the lowest estimate, and possibly a much greater distance.

One moonlight night a little later, while we were traveling under short sail with considerable ice about, a whale blew a short distance to windward. I was at the wheel and Mr. Landers was standing near me.

"Blow!" breathed Mr. Landers softly. Suddenly the whale breached—we could hear it distinctly as it shot up from a narrow channel between ice floes. "There she breaches!" said Mr. Landers in the same low voice, with no particular concern. We thought the big creature merely was enjoying a moonlight frolic. It breached again. This time its body crashed upon a strip of ice and flopped and floundered for a moment before sliding back into the water. Then it breached half a dozen times more in rapid succession. I had never seen a whale breach more than once at a time, even when wounded.

Mr. Landers became interested. "I wonder what's the matter with that whale," he said.

To our surprise, two other black bodies began to flash up into the moonlight about the whale. Every time the whale breached, they breached, too. They were of huge size, but nothing like so large as the whale.

"Killers!" cried Mr. Landers excitedly.

Then we knew the whale was not playing, but fighting for its life. It leaped above the surface to a lesser and lesser height each time. Plainly it was tiring fast. When it breached the last time only its head and a small portion of its body rose into the air and both killers seemed to be hanging with a bulldog grip upon its lower jaw. What the outcome of that desperate battle was we did not see. The whale and its savage assailants moved off out of eyeshot. But for some time after we had lost sight of the whale we could hear its labored and stertoreous breathing and its heavy splashes as it attempted to breach.

Killers, Mr. Landers told me, are themselves a species of rapacious, carnivorous whale, whose upper and lower jaws are armed with sharp, saw-like teeth. They are otherwise known as the Orca gladiator, and tiger-hearted gladiators of the sea they are. The great, clumsy bowhead with no teeth with which to defend itself, whose only weapons are its flukes and its fins, is no match for them. They attack the great creature whenever they encounter it, and when it has exhausted itself in its efforts to escape, they tear open its jaws and feast upon its tongue. The killer whale never hunts alone. It pursues its titanic quarry in couples and trios, and sometimes in veritable wolf-like packs of half a dozen. There is usually no hope for the bowhead that these relentless creatures mark for their prey.

22

The Stranded Whale

OUR fourth and last whale gave us quite a bit of trouble. We sighted this fellow spouting in a choppy sea among ice islands two or three miles off the edges of the polar pack. All three boats lowered for it. It was traveling slowly in the same direction the brig was sailing and about two miles from the vessel. It took the boats some time to work to close quarters. When the mate's boat was almost within striking distance, the whale went under. As frightened whales usually run against the wind, Mr. Winchester steered to windward. But the whale had not been frightened; it had not seen the boats. Consequently it failed to head into the wind, but did the unexpected by coming up to leeward, blowing with evident unconcern. This brought it nearest to Gabriel, who went after it in a flash. After a sharp, swift run down the wind, we struck the whale, which dived and went racing under water for the ice pack. The dizzy rate at which it took out our line might have led us to believe it was not hurt, but we knew it was seriously wounded by the fountains of blood it sent up whenever it came to the surface.

The captain's signals from the brig, by this time, had headed the other boats in our direction, but they could not reach us in time to be of any assistance. The whale ran away with our tub of line and we sat still and watched the red fountains that marked its course as it headed for the big ice to the north.

Directly in the whale's course lay an ice floe about half a mile long, a few hundred yards wide and rising from five to ten feet above the surface. We naturally supposed the creature would dive under this and keep going for the main pack. To our surprise we soon saw fountain after fountain, red with blood, shooting up from the center of the floe. The whale evidently was too badly injured to continue its flight and had sought refuge beneath this strip of drifting ice.

Men were hurriedly landed from all the boats with harpoons and shoulder guns, leaving enough sailors on the thwarts to fend the boats clear of the ice. The landing parties clambered over the broken and tumbled ice, dragging the harpoon lines. We found the whale half exposed in a narrow opening in the center of the floe, all the ice about it red with clotted blood. Long John and Little Johnny threw two harpoons each into the big body and Big Foot Louis threw his remaining one. As a result of this bombardment, five tonite bombs exploded in the whale, which, with the harpoons sticking all over its back, suggested a baited bull in a Spanish bullring hung with the darts of the banderilleros. But the great animal kept on breathing blood and would not die. After all the harpoons had been exhausted, shoulder guns were brought into play. In all, twelve tonite bombs were fired into it before the monster gave a mighty shiver and lay still.

But with the whale dead, we still had a big problem on our hands. In some way the giant bulk had to be hauled out of the ice. This was a difficult matter even with plenty of time in which to do it. Night was coming on and it was the brig's custom in the hours of darkness to sail far away from the great ice pack with its edging of floating bergs and floes in order to avoid possible accident and to sail back to the whaling grounds on the morrow.

This Captain Shorey prepared to do now. As a solution of the dilemma, an empty bread cask or hogshead was brought on deck and the name of the brig was seared in its staves with a hot iron in several places. This cask was towed to the floe, hauled up on the edge of the ice, and the long line of one of the harpoons sticking in the whale was made fast to it by means of staples. Thus the cask marked the floe in which the whale was lying.

It was growing dark when the brig went about, said good-night to the whale, and headed for open water to the south. We sailed away before a stiff breeze and soon cask and floe and the great white continent beyond had faded from view. When morning broke we were bowling along under light sail in a choppy sea with nothing but water to be seen in any direction. The great ice cap was somewhere out of sight over the world's northern rim. Not a floe, a berg, or the smallest white chunk of ice floated anywhere in the purple sphere of sea ringed by the wide horizon.

Being a green hand, I said to myself, "Good-bye, Mr. Whale, we certainly have seen the last we'll ever see of you."

Let me make the situation perfectly clear. Our whale was drifting somewhere about the Arctic Ocean embedded in an ice floe scarcely to be distinguished from a thousand other floes except by a cask upon its margin which at a distance of a few miles would hardly be visible through strong marine glasses. The floe, remember, was not a stationary object whose longitude and latitude could be reckoned certainly, but was being tossed about by the sea and driven by the winds and ocean currents.

The brig, on the other hand, had been sailing on the wind without a set course. It had been tacking and wearing from time to time. It, too, had felt the compulsion of the waves and currents. So throughout the night the brig had sailed at random and twenty miles or so away the whale in its floe had been drifting at random. Now how were we going to find our whale again? This struck me that morning on the open sea with neither whale nor ice in sight, as a problem certainly very nice, if not hopeless. The way it was solved was as pretty a feat of navigation as I ever saw.

When Captain Shorey came on deck after breakfast, he "shot the sun" through his sextant and went below to make his calculations. In a little while he came on deck again and stepped to the man at the wheel. The helmsman was steering full and by.

"How do you head?" asked Captain Shorey.

"Northwest," answered the sailor.

"Keep her northwest by west half west," said the captain.

For several hours the brig sailed steadily on this course. Along about nine o'clock, we saw the peculiar, cold, light look above the sky line ahead which meant ice and which sailors call an "ice horizon," to be distinguished at a glance from a water horizon, which is dark. A little later, we sighted the white loom of the great ice continent. Later still, we picked up the bergs, floes, islands, and chunks of ice which drift forever along its edge.

The brig kept on its course. A floe of ice, looking at a distance like a long, narrow ribbon, lay ahead of us, apparently directly across our path. As we drew nearer, we began to make out dimly a certain dark speck upon the edge of the ice. This speck gradually assumed definiteness. It was our cask and we were headed straight for it. To a landlubber unacquainted with the mysteries of navigation, this incident may seem almost unbelievable, but upon my honest word, it is true to the last detail.

After the brig had been laid aback near the ice, a boat was lowered and a hole was cut in the bow of the whale's head. A cable was passed through this and the other end was made fast aboard the ship. Then under light sail, the brig set about the work of pulling the whale out of the ice. The light breeze fell away and the three boats were strung out ahead with hawsers and lent assistance with the oars. It was slow work. But when the breeze freshened, the ice began gradually to give, then to open up, and finally the whale was hauled clear and drawn alongside for the cutting in.

23

And So—Home

IT was on October tenth that we broke out the Stars and Stripes at our main gaff and squared our yards for home. Everybody cheered as the flag went fluttering up, for everybody was glad that the end of the long, hard voyage was in sight. Bering Straits which when we were about to enter the Arctic Ocean—sea of tragedy and graveyard of so many brave men and tall ships—had looked like the portals of inferno, now when we were homeward bound seemed like the gateway to the Happy Isles.

The four whales we had captured on the voyage had averaged about 1,800 pounds of baleen, which that year was quoted at $6.50 a pound. We had tried out all our whales except the last one and our casks were filled with oil. Our entire catch was worth over $50,000. The officers and boat-steerers made a pretty penny out of the voyage. The captain, I was told, had shipped on a lay of one-sixth—and got it. The sailors had shipped on the 190th lay—and didn't get it. That was the difference. At San Francisco, the forecastle hands were paid off with the "big iron dollar" of whaling tradition.

The homeward voyage was not a time of idleness. We were kept busy a large part of the time cleaning the bone of our last three whales—the bone from our first whale had been shipped to San Francisco from Unalaska. As we had at first stowed it away, the baleen was in bunches of ten or a dozen slabs held together at the roots by "white horse," which is the whaler name for the gums of the whale. These bunches were now brought up on deck and each slab of baleen was cut out of the gums separately and washed and scoured with cocoanut rind procured for the purpose in the Hawaiian Islands. Then the slabs were dried and polished until they shone like gun metal, tied into bales, and stowed under hatches once more.

A little south of King's Island in the northern end of Bering Sea, Captain Shorey set a course for Unimak Pass. We ran down Bering Sea with a gale of wind sweeping us before it and great billows bearing us along. When we bore up for the dangerous passage which had given us such a scare in the spring, we were headed straight for it, and we went through into the Pacific without pulling a rope. It was another remarkable example of the navigating skill of whaling captains. We had aimed at Unimak Pass when 700 miles away and had scored a bull's-eye.

Again the "roaring forties" lived up to their name and buffeted us with gale and storm. The first land we sighted after leaving the Fox Islands was the wooded hills of northern California. I shall never forget how beautiful those hills appeared and what a welcome they seemed to hold out. They were my own country again, the United States—home. My eyes grew misty as I gazed at them and I felt much as a small boy might feel who, after long absence, sees his mother's arms open to him. The tug that picked us up outside of Golden Gate at sundown one day seemed like a long lost friend. It was long after darkness had fallen, that it towed us into San Francisco harbor, past the darkly frowning Presidio and the twinkling lights of Telegraph Hill, to an anchorage abreast the city, brilliantly lighted and glowing like fairyland. I never in all my life heard sweeter music than the rattle and clank of the anchor chain as the great anchor plunged into the bay and sank to its grip in good American soil once more.

My whaling voyage was over. It was an adventure out of the ordinary, an experience informing, interesting, health-giving, and perhaps worth while. I have never regretted it. But I wouldn't do it again for ten thousand dollars.

THE END

About The Author

Walter Noble Burns was born in 1872. After responding to a help wanted ad he shipped out on the whaling bark *Alexander* in 1890.Sorely tested during his adventures in the Bering Sea, Burns published this memoir in 1913, long after he had left the *Alexander*, never to set foot on a whaler again.

HISTORICAL MEMOIRS FROM 1500 BOOKS

The Private Life of Marie Antoinette by Madame Campan—An intimate account of the intrigue and drama of the royal court from the Queen's trusted Lady-in-Waiting.

A Minstrel In France by Harry Lauder—A world famous performer's life is forever changed by the loss of his beloved son in World War I. With a piano lashed to his jeep Lauder tours the battle-front in France paying tribute to the troops.

A Year With A Whaler by Walter Noble Burns—The stories of the able-bodied seamen, the great mammals, and the ever changing sea are the central figures in this narrative of a carefree boy shipping out and a wise man returning.

Thirty Years A Detective by Allan Pinkerton—
From the founder of the Pinkerton agency an
insider's look at criminals, their mindsets, and their
most famous schemes.

**A New Voyage Round the World by William
Dampier**—A fascinating travelogue, a scientific
journey, and a buccaneering adventure from
Dampier—gentleman sailor and pirate.

To Cuba and Back by Richard Henry Dana—The
best-selling author's account of his 1859 trip to the
tropical island where colonial expansionism and
slavery meet head on.

"The best memoirs in any language…
a supreme masterpiece"
The Sunday Times

Memoirs of
Duc de
Saint-Simon
Available Fall 2007

Edited and translated from the French by
Lucy Norton

"Miss Norton has caught Saint-Simon alive…an
English classic."
Nancy Mitford

"Written with wit, poignancy and total frankness…."
Auberon Waugh

Warwick, NY

Excerpt from

THIRTY YEARS A
DETECTIVE

by

ALLAN PINKERTON

The Pickpocket

IF we trace the career of the professional criminal to its incipiency, it will almost invariably be found that the first plunge into the vortex of crime has been that of pocket-picking. Among the alarming number of professional thieves of all grades in the country to-day, it would be difficult to find one who had not at the commencement of his dishonest experience, been engaged in picking the pockets of the innocent and the unsuspecting. It is equally true also that of all the departments of crime as now practiced there is not one which contains a larger number of adept operators than that of pickpockets. In almost every crowded assembly they will assuredly be found. They follow the circuits of the racing season; they are hangers on about the traveling circus; are to be found at the theatres, and in the church. At mass meetings, at merry makings and even at funerals, this pestilent thief obtrudes himself, and dismay and loss inevitably follow his appearance.

The grades of this class of criminals are exceedingly numerous, and range from the ragged urchin who steals a pocket-handkerchief to the expert professional who can with ease and safety remove a well-filled wallet from the inside coat pocket of his hapless victim. The intermediate grades are well defined, and vary according to the skillfulness and daring of the thieves themselves. In this branch of crime women as well as men are active workers, and many of the female thieves are as successful as the men, in the ease and grace with which they relieve the unsuspecting of their valuables. There are some male thieves who confine their operations entirely to ladies, and there are others who could not be induced to rob a lady under any circumstances whatever. The female thieves operate indiscriminately, although they are more successful with ladies than with gentlemen. In the accepted language of the thief, those who operate on men are termed "Bloke-buzzers," while those who make ladies their special victims receive the euphonious appellation of "Moll-buzzers."

A description of the means resorted to by the fraternity of pickpockets may prove both interesting and instructive, and as I have had a large experience with all classes of this community, I will endeavor to describe their operations for the benefit of suffering humanity.

In order to give due prominence even to questionable merit, I will begin by detailing the operations of the more ambitious of the male pickpockets, those who frequent the localities where the large banking institutions are situated, and endeavor to rob those who are entering or leaving the banks. For the accomplishment of success in work of this nature, four men usually travel together, who are generally called "a mob." The man who is to do the actual stealing is called the "tool," or "hook," and the others are known as "stalls."

After selecting their victim or "mark," who is engaged in drawing a large sum of money from the bank, one of the number will take up his position inside of the bank, where he can watch every movement of the man who is to be robbed. This is done in order to ascertain exactly where the money is placed, so that no delay may ensue in locating the desired "plunder." Having acquired the necessary information, the "stall" will inform his companions on the sidewalk in which pocket the money is secured, and they then proceed to business. As a general rule, a man who draws several packages of bills from a bank, will place them in his inside coat pocket, and in this instance we will assume that the person who has excited the cupidity of the thieves, has placed his money in the inside pocket on the right side of the coat. He emerges from the bank, reaches the sidewalk, and proceeds upon his way. The thieves follow him within easy distance, but will not make any attempt to accomplish their purpose unless they notice that he is about to enter a crowded thoroughfare, a car, a narrow street, or through a hallway into a building. If in a crowd or narrow street the thieves will, without any preliminary notice whatever, act as follows: Two of the "stalls" will immediately manage to get in front of the man—and these men are called "front stalls"—this is done for the purpose of stopping him or blocking his way for a moment when the time arrives. The "tool" or "hook" will also get slightly ahead of the man, and when the moment for action arrives a slight cough will bring the two "front stalls" to a stand-still. This, of course, impedes the progress of the victim. Quick as a flash, and yet with an ease of motion that attracts no particular attention, the "tool" turns sideways, almost facing the man, but upon his right side. The "tool" usually carries a coat upon his arm for the purpose of covering his hand; with the concealed hand he will work under the man's coat, and taking the wallet or package by the top, will raise it straight up, until it is entirely clear of the pocket; then drawing it under his own coat, the robbery is complete. During this operation, which requires but a few seconds, the "stall" behind the man is pushing and shoving him repeatedly on the left side, as if with the intention of getting past him. The left side being furthest from where the money is concealed, answers two purposes: it not only serves to prevent the man from feeling or detecting the easy sliding motion of the wallet as it is being drawn out of his pocket on the other side, and it at the same time helps to turn the man more toward the "tool" or "hook," so that his work is rendered easier. While this operation is going on the two "front stalls" have not betrayed the slightest interest in the proceedings, and from all appearances are entirely ignorant of the fact that a man is being deliberately robbed behind them. They have not so much as turned their heads, and consequently do not know when the operation is completed, so that they may stand aside and let the victim pass. In order to overcome this, the pickpockets have adopted certain words or signals, which are thoroughly understood by the craft, and these signals are given by the "tool" or "hook." If he is rather slow about getting to the wallet or the money, and he notices that the front men are getting somewhat uneasy, he calls out "stick!" This means that in a few seconds he will be successful, and that they are to stay in their respective positions. After he has secured the wallet he will chirp like a bird, or will utter the word "lam!" This means to let the man go, and to get out of the way as soon as possible. This word is also used in case the money cannot be taken, and further attempts are useless.

It sometimes happens that it is somewhat difficult to get the wallet or package out of the pocket, and if any unusual force is used in withdrawing it, the man will feel it, and give an alarm. In cases of this kind, the "tool," when he has the wallet in his fingers and ready to be drawn out, will cry, "Rouse!" At this signal all of the "stalls" give the man a general push at the same time, and during the confusion of the moment, the "tool" deftly pulls out the wallet and decamps.

While the detailing of this operation has taken some time, the operation itself is performed in a few seconds, and in almost every instance, without attracting the attention or exciting the suspicion of the individual who is so ruthlessly despoiled of his money.

As a general rule a merchant who goes himself, or sends his clerk to the bank to make a deposit, places the money and checks lengthwise in his bank book, which is generally shorter than the notes, and allows them to project beyond the edges of the book. The book is then placed in the inside pocket and so carried to the bank. A man is usually suspicious and careful when he is entrusted with a large sum of money and the thieves have therefore to be very careful in their manipulations. When a gentleman thus engaged, is subjected to a crowding or pushing from others, he naturally places his hand upon the book, which contains his money, in order to be assured of its safety. The thieves are perfectly aware of this, and when the opportunity offers they simply seize the ends of the bills which extend beyond the book, and by a quick and dexterous motion extract the money and leave the book remaining in the pocket. As a natural result, when the suspicious depositor by feeling upon the outside, finds his book safely bestowed within, he gives no thought to the fact that he has been robbed and does not discover his misfortune until he reaches the bank. This process is called by the thieves "weeding."

There are some people who imagine that it is an impossibility for a thief to rob them, and they are ever on the alert. These, people place their bank book and money in the outside pocket of their sack-coat, and by keeping their hand upon the book imagine that a robbery is impossible. The thieves, however, know better than this, and their mode of proceeding is as follows.

They patiently bide their time until the man reaches the door of the bank, which must be opened to admit him—one man will then step immediately in front of him, or a little to the left—and then stop right in front of the doorway pretending to look at a paper, or, to count some money which he has in his hands—the consequence is, that instead of pushing the man aside so he can use his left hand to open the door—the victim will, unthinkingly, reach out his right hand—which had hitherto guarded his pocket, and pull open the door—the "stall" immediately moves a trifle more to the front for a second, and then turns away—that second, however, is enough, for while the victim and his "stall" are thus engaged, the pickpocket has quietly taken out the money and decamped. This in thieves vernacular is called a "tale trick" and bank messengers have frequently been robbed in this manner.

Should the money be carried in the pockets of the pantaloons, the methods are, of course, different. This style of robbery is much more difficult, and as a general thing is not so remunerative as stealing from men who are either going to or returning from the bank. The thieves who follow this branch of their calling are as a class more rude and rough in their appearance and nature, and their actions, while at work, are more abrupt and harsh.

This kind of robbery is generally practiced on the cars—called "rattlers"—or in a crowd—and if upon the cars is performed on the platforms or in the doorways of these crowded vehicles.

It may be as well to state that among thieves certain terms are used to represent articles which otherwise have proper names. A pocket-book is called "leather"; a wallet "a pittman" or "pitt"; a pocket is called a "kick"; hands are termed "dukes"; a handkerchief a "wipe," and a hat is dubbed a "tile."

The thieves of this latter class will generally select for their victim—which they call a "mark"—an elderly man, or one who appears to hail from the country. The first are usually more feeble and not supposed to be as sharp as a young man—while the countryman is supposed to carry more ready money about with him than a person belonging to the city.

The pickpockets board a street car and take their positions on the rear platform—always being careful to select a car which is already crowded. For the purpose of illustration we will assume that there is an individual on the platform who looks as if he might have some money in his pocket-book. The first thing to be done is to ascertain in which pocket the money is carried, and to do this the thief lightly runs his hand across the front of both pockets of the "mark"—and this operation of feeling for a pocket-book is called "fanning." Should the pocket-book be found in the left pocket, the "tool" will say to his companions "left kick," and this will inform them all where the money is located. The "stalls" then surround the "mark," and the "tool" begins to work. With his hand covered with a coat over his arm, he inserts the two first fingers of his right hand, just beyond the first joint—into the victim's pocket, with the inside of the fingers against the pocket lining farthest from the body. First bending one finger and then the other, he draws the pocket up little by little, which is known as "reefing," until the pocket-book is drawn up within reach. The moment he is able to take hold of the pocket-book, called "tapping," he quietly calls out "Rouse!" the victim receives a rough push from the stalls and out comes the pocket-book, which is at once passed to one of the stalls. This is done to guard against accidental discovery, for should the victim miss his money and accuse the "tool" of the theft, he will not find the book upon him, and that is generally sufficient to enable him to get off. The "stall" requires to be informed when the pocket-book is taken, and he waits for the "tool" to whisper "collar this!" or to chirp like a bird, when he knows that he is to receive the money, and that the robbery has been success-fully ended.

In some cases, particularly among persons from the country, the travelers have heard remarkable stories about the picking of pockets, and have made up their minds that such a fate shall not befall them. To make sure of this they invariably travel about with their hands in their pockets and on top their purses. This careful and watchful traveler gets on a street car, and the pickpockets at once select him as their "mark." He is immediately pressed and hemmed in by the gang, and the hand that is not religiously guarding the treasure in his pocket is kept back by the shoulder of one of the stalls. A quiet command "tile him!" is given, and the countryman's hat is shoved forward from behind. The countryman, not being able to use his other arm, pulls his hand out of his pocket and secures his hat. As soon as this is done, one of the "stalls" gets into position, and places his shoulder under the countryman's arm, thus preventing him for a moment from again placing his hand in his pocket. In a second the "tool" is at work, and in another moment the gentleman from the country finds plenty of room on the platform, for the thieves have left, and with them has disappeared his carefully guarded pocket-book.

When all the seats in a street car are occupied, a pickpocket will occasionally enter and take up a standing position in front of some gentleman who has his coat open. Hanging by one hand to the strap suspended from the roof of the car, and with a coat thrown over his other arm, he will attempt a robbery. Swaying about with the motion of the car, he manages it so that his coat will come directly under the chin of the seated passenger, and under cover of that, he will extract a pocket-book from the inside pocket of the man, who has no suspicion of what is going on. Diamond studs of great value have frequently been taken from the bosoms of unsus-pecting passengers under the cover of a coat or newspaper, which the standing pickpocket manages to place under the chin of his victim, apparently caused by the motion of the car. If a diamond stud with a screw is to be taken, the thief after covering the stud with his coat or newspaper, will gently take hold of the screw with his thumb and forefinger, and draw the bosom of the shirt away from the body of the victim—the thumb nail is then inserted immediately back of the head of the screw and then with a firm twist or turn of the hand, the screw will come out. No matter how difficult this operation appears under ordinary circumstances, it will invariably yield to the application of the thumb under the setting of the stone. Should the diamond be set with a flat back instead of a screw, it is impossible to detach it from the bosom, and the thief will instantly desist from further efforts to remove it. A diamond pin is unfastened in the natural way and then raised up straight. A pin or screw stud is generally called a "prop," by the thieves.

Should the pickpockets attempt to work upon a railroad train, they generally select their victim in advance, by watching at the ticket office and noticing a prospective passenger who exhibits a large amount of money. Should no favorable opportunity occur to rob him while he is getting on the car, the thieves will wait until he is quietly seated, when one of their number will approach him, and in a voice of authority inquire:

"Where is your ticket for?"

The passenger, supposing his questioner to be a railroad official, will at once inform him, when the thief will reply:

"Then you must take the next car," indicating either the car in front or in the rear, at the same time picking up the traveler's valise, with a view of assisting him in effecting the change, and calling out, "Come on, sir!"

The man follows obediently, and the mob is waiting for him on the platform. As soon as he appears he is at once jammed in, and robbed. Their previous knowledge of the location of his money renders their task an easy and rapid one, and the robbery is effected in a flash.

Excerpt from

A NEW VOYAGE
ROUND THE
WORLD

by

WILLIAM DAMPIER

This Boca-toro is a place that the privateers use to resort to, as much as any place on all the coast, because here is plenty of green tortoise, and a good careening place. The Indians here have no commerce with the Spaniards; but are very barbarous, and will not be dealt with. They have destroyed many privateers, as they did not long after this some of Captain Pain's men; who having built a tent ashore to put his goods in while he careened his ship, and some men lying there with their arms, in the night the Indians crept softly into the tent, and cut off the heads of 3 or 4 men, and made their escape; nor was this the first time they had served the privateers so. There grow on this coast vinelloes in great quantity, with which chocolate is perfumed. These I shall describe elsewhere.

Our fleet being thus scattered, there were now no hopes of getting together again; therefore every one did what they thought most conducing to obtain their ends. Captain Wright, with whom I now was, was resolved to cruise on the Coast of Cartagene; and it being now almost the Westerly wind season, we sailed from hence, and Captain Yanky with us; and we consorted, because Captain Yanky had no commission, and was afraid the French would take away his bark. We passed by Scuda, a small island (where 'tis said Sir Francis Drake's bowels were buried) and came to a small river to Westward of Chagre; where we took two new canoes, and carried them with us into the Sambaloes. We had the wind at West, with much rain; which brought us to Point-Samballas. Here Captain Wright and Captain Yanky left us in the tartane, to fix the canoes, while they went on the coast of Cartagene to seek for provision. We cruised in among the islands, and kept our Moskito men, or strikers, out, who brought aboard some half-grown tortoise; and some of us went ashore every day to hunt for what we could find in the woods: sometimes we got peccary, warree, or deer; at other times we light on a drove of large fat monkeys, or quames, corrosoes, (each a large sort of fowl) pigeons, parrots, or turtle-doves. We lived very well on what we got, not staying long in one place; but sometimes we would go on the islands, where there grow great groves of sapadillies, which is a sort of fruit much like a pear, but more juicy; and under those trees we found plenty of soldiers, a little kind of animals that live in shells and have two great claws like a crab, and are good food. One time our men found a great many large ones, and being sharp-set had them dressed, but most of them were very sick afterwards, being poisoned by them: for on this island were many manchaneel trees, whose fruit is like a small crab, and smells very well, but they are not wholesome; and we commonly take care of meddling with any animals that eat them. And this we take for a general rule, when we find any fruits that we have not seen before, if we see them pecked by birds, we may freely eat, but if we see no such sign, we let them alone; for of this fruit no birds will taste. Many of these islands have of these manchaneel trees growing on them.

Thus cruising in among these islands, at length we came again to La Sound's Key; and the day before having met with a Jamaica sloop that was come over on the coast to trade, she went with us. It was in the evening when we came to an anchor, and the next morning we fired two guns for the Indians that lived on the main to come aboard; for by this time we concluded we should hear from our five men, that we left in the heart of the country among the Indians, this being about the latter end of August, and it was the beginning of May when we parted from them. According to our expectation the Indians came aboard, and brought our friends with them: Mr. Wafer wore a clout about him, and was painted like an Indian; and he was some time aboard before I knew him. One of them, named Richard Cobson, died within 3 or 4 day's after, and was buried on La Sound's Key.

After this we went to other keys, to the Eastward of these, to meet Captain Wright and Captain Yanky, who met with a fleet of pereagoes laden with Indian corn, hog, and fowls, going to Cartagene; being convoyed by a small armadilly of 2 guns and 6 patereroes. Her they chased ashore, and most of the pereagoes; but they got two of them off, and brought them away.

Here Captain Wright's and Captain Yanky's barks were cleaned; and we stocked our selves with corn, and then went towards the coast of Cartagene. In our way thither we passed by the river of Darien; which is very broad at the mouth, but not above six foot water on a Spring-tide; for the tide riseth but little here. Captain Coxon, about 6 months before we came out of the South Seas, went up this river with a party of men: every man carried a small strong bag to put his gold in; expecting great riches there, though they got little or none. They rowed up about 100 leagues before they came to any settlement, and then found some Spaniards, who lived there to truck with the Indians for gold; there being gold scales in every house. The Spaniards admired how they came so far from the mouth of the river, because there are a sort of Indians living between that place and the sea, who are very dreadful to the Spaniards, and will not have any commerce with them, nor with any white people. They use trunks about 8 foot long, out of which they blow poisoned darts; and are so silent in their attacks on their enemies, and retreat so nimbly again, that the Spaniards can never find them. Their darts are made of macaw-wood, being about the bigness and length of a knitting-needle; one end is wound about with cotton, the other end is extraordinary sharp and small; and is jagged with notches like a harpoon: so that whatever it strikes into, it immediately breaks off, by the weight of the biggest end; which it is not of strength to bear, (it being made so slender for that purpose) and is very difficult to be got out again, by reason of those notches. These Indians have always war with our Darien friendly Indians, and live on both sides this great river 50 or 60 leagues from the sea, but not near the mouth of the river. There are abundance of manatee in this river, and some creeks belonging to it. This relation I had from several men who accompanied Captain Coxon in that discovery; and from Mr. Cook in particular, who was with them, and is a very intelligent person: He is now chief mate of a ship bound to Guinea. To return therefore to the prosecution of our voyage; meeting with nothing of note, we passed by Cartagene; which is a city so well known, that I shall say nothing of it. We sailed by in sight of it, for it lies open to the sea: and had a fair view of Madre de Popa, or Nuestra Sennora de Popa, a monastery of the Virgin Mary's, standing on the top of a very steep hill just behind Cartagene. It is a place of incredible wealth, by reason of the offerings made here continually; and for this reason often in danger of being visited by the privateers, did not the neighbourhood of Cartagene, keep them in awe. 'Tis in short, the very Loretto of the West Indies: it hath innumerable miracles related of it. Any misfortune that befalls the rivateers is attributed to this Lady's doing; and the Spaniards report that she was abroad that night the *Oxford* man-of-war was blown up at the Isle of Vacca near Hispaniola, and that she came home all wet; as, belike, she often returns with her clothes dirty and torn with passing through woods, and bad ways, when she has been out upon any expedition; deserving doubtless a new suit for such eminent pieces of service.

From hence we passed on to the Rio Grande, where we took up fresh water at sea, a league off the mouth of that river. From thence we sailed eastward, passing by St. Martha, a large town, and good harbour, belonging to the Spaniards: yet hath it within these few years been twice taken by the privateers. It stands close upon the sea, and the hill within land is a very large one, towering up a great heighth from a vast body of land. I am of opinion that it is higher than the Pike of Tenariff; others also that have seen both think the same; though its bigness makes its heighth less sensible. I have seen it in passing by, 30 leagues off at sea; others, as they told me, above 60: and several have told me, that they have seen at once, Jamaica, Hispaniola, and the high Land of Santa Martha; and yet the nearest of these two places is distant from it 120 leagues; and Jamaica, which is farthest off, is accounted near 150 leagues; and I question whether any land on either of those two islands may be seen 50 leagues. Its head is generally hid in the clouds; but in clear weather, when the top appears, it looks white; supposed to be covered with snow. St. Martha lieth in the Lat. of 12 Deg. North.

Being advanced 5 or 6 leagues to the Eastward of Santa Martha, we left our ships at anchor, and returned back in our canoes to the River Grande; entering it by a mouth of it that disembogues it self near Santa Martha: purposing to attempt some towns that lie a pretty way up that river. But this design meeting with discouragements, we returned to our ships, and set sail to Rio la Hacha. This hath been a strong Spanish town, and is well built; but being often taken by the privateers, the Spaniards deserted it some time before our arrival. It lieth to the Westward of a river; and right against the town is a good road for ships, the bottom clean, and sandy. The Jamaica sloops used often to come over to trade here: and I am informed that the Spaniards have again settled themselves in it, and made it very strong. We entered the fort, and brought two small guns aboard. From thence we went to the rancheries, one or two small Indian villages, where the Spaniards keep two barks to fish for pearl. The pearl-banks lie about 4 or 5 leagues off from the shore, as I have been told; thither the fishing-barks go and anchor; then the divers go down to the bottom, and fill a basket (which is let down before) with oysters; and when they come up, others go down, two at a time; this they do till the bark is full, and then go ashore, where the old men, women and children of the Indians open the oysters, there being a Spanish overseer to look after the pearl. Yet these Indians do very often secure the best pearl for themselves, as many Jamaica-men can testify who daily trade with them. The meat they string up, and hang it a drying. At this place we went ashore, where we found one of the barks, and saw great heaps of oyster-shells, but the people all fled: yet in another place, between this and Rio La Hacha, we took some of the Indians, who seem to be a stubborn sort of people: they are long visaged, black hair, their noses somewhat rising in the middle, and of a stern look. The Spaniards report them to be a very numerous nation; and that they will not subject themselves to their yoke. Yet they have Spanish priests among them; and by trading have brought them to be somewhat sociable;

but cannot keep a severe hand over them. The land is but barren, it being of light sand near the sea; and most savannah, or champaign; and the grass but thin and course, yet they feed plenty of cattle. Every man knoweth his own, and looketh after them; but the land is in common, except only their houses or small plantations where they live, which every man maintains with some fence about it. They may remove from one place to another as they please, no man having right to any land but what he possesseth. This part of the country is not so subject to rain as to the Westward of Santa Martha; yet here are tornadoes, or thunder-showers; but neither so violent as on the coast of Portabell, nor so frequent. The Westerly winds in the Westerly wind season blow here, though not so strong nor lasting as on the coasts of Cartagene and Portabell.

When we had spent some time here, we returned again towards the coast of Cartagene; and being between Rio Grande and that place, we met with Westerly winds, which kept us still to the Eastward of Cartagene 3 or 4 days; and then in the morning we descried a sail off at sea, and we chased her at noon: Captain Wright, who sailed best, came up with her, and engaged her; and in half an hour after Captain Yanky, who sailed better than the tartan (the vessel that I was in) came up with her likewise, and laid her aboard, then Captain Wright also; and they took her before we came up. They lost 2 or 3 men, and had 7 or 8 wounded. The prize was a ship of 12 guns and 40 men, who had all good small arms: she was laden with sugar and tobacco, and had 8 or 10 tons of marmalade on board: she came from Saint Jago on Cuba, and was bound to Cartagene.

We went back with her to Rio Grande, to fix our rigging which was shattered in the fight, and to consider what to do with her; for these were commodities of little use to us, and not worth going into a port with. At the Rio Grande Captain Wright demanded the prize as his due by virtue of his commission: Captain Yanky said it was his due by the Law of Privateers. Indeed Captain Wright had the most right to her, having by his commission protected Captain Yanky from the French, who would have turned him out because he had no commission; and he likewise began to engage her first. But the company were all afraid that Captain Wright would presently carry her into a port; therefore most of Captain Wright's men stuck to Captain Yanky, and Captain Wright losing his prize burned his own bark, and had

Captain Yanky's, it being bigger than his own;
the tartan was sold to a Jamaica trader, and
Captain Yanky commanded the prize ship.
We went again from hence to Rio la Hacha,
and set the prisoners ashore; and it being now
the beginning of November, we concluded to
go to Querisao to sell our sugar, if favoured
by westerly winds, which were now come in.
We sailed from thence, having fair weather
and winds to our mind, which brought us to
Querisao, a Dutch island. Captain Wright
went ashore to the Governour, and offered him
the sale of the sugar: but the Governour told
him he had a great trade with the Spaniards,
therefore he could not admit us in there; but if
we would go to St. Thomas, which is an island,
and free port, belonging to the Danes, and a
sanctuary for privateers, he would send a sloop
with such goods as we wanted, and money to
buy the sugar, which he would take at a certain
rate; but it was not agreed to.

Querisao is the only island of importance
that the Dutch have in the West Indies. It is
about 5 leagues in length, and may be 9 or 10
in circumference: the northernmost point is
laid down in North lat. 12 d. 40 m. and it is
about 7 or 8 leagues from the main, near Cape
Roman. On the South side of the East end is

a good harbour, called Santa Barbara; but the chiefest harbour, is about 3 leagues from the S. E. end, on the South side of it where the Dutch have a very good town, and a very strong fort. Ships bound in thither must be sure to keep close to the harbour's mouth, and have a hasar, or rope ready to send one end ashore to the fort: for there is no anchoring at the entrance of the harbour, and the current always sets to the Westward. But being got in, it is a very secure port for ships, either to careen, or lie safe. At the East end are two hills, one of them is much higher than the other, and steepest towards the North side. The rest of the island is indifferent level; where of late some rich men have made sugar works; which formerly was all pasture for cattle: there are also some small plantations of potatoes and yams, and they have still a great many cattle on the island; but it is not so much esteemed for its produce, as for its situation for the trade with the Spaniard. Formerly the harbour was never without ships from Cartagene and Portabell, that did use to buy of the Dutch here 1000 or 1500 negroes at once, besides great quantities of European commodities; but of late that trade is fallen into the hands of the English at Jamaica: yet still the Dutch have a vast trade over all the West

Indies, sending from Holland ships of good force laden with European goods, whereby they make very profitable returns. The Dutch have two other Islands here, but of little moment in comparison of Querisao; the one lieth 7 or 8 leagues to the Westward of Querisao, called Aruba; the other 9 or 10 leagues to the Eastward of it, called Bon-Airy. From these Islands the Dutch fetch in sloops provision for Querisao, to maintain their garrison and negroes. I was never at Aruba, therefore cannot say any thing of it as to my own knowledge; but by report it is much, like Bon-Airy, which I shall describe, only not so big. Between Querisao and Bon-Airy is a small Island called Little Querisao, it is not above a league from Great Querisao. The King of France has long had an eye on Querisao, and made some attempts to take it, but never yet succeeded. I have heard that about 23 or 24 years since the Governour had sold it to the French, but died a small time before the fleet came to demand it, and by his death that design failed. Afterwards, in the year 1678, the Count d' Estre, who a year before had taken the Isle of Tobago from the Dutch, was sent hither also with a squadron of stout ships, very well manned, and fitted with bombs and carcasses intending to take it by storm.

This fleet first came to Martinico; where, while they stayed, orders were sent to Petit Guaves, for all privateers to repair thither, and assist the Count in his design. There were but two privateer's ships that went thither to him, which were manned partly with French, partly with Englishmen. These set out with the Count; but in their way to Querisao, the whole fleet was lost on a riff or ridge of rocks, that runs off from the Isle of Aves; not above two ships escaping, one of which was one of the privateers; and so that design perished.

Wherefore not driving a bargain for our sugar with the Governour of Querisao, we went from thence to Bon-Airy, another Dutch Island, where we met a Dutch sloop come from Europe, laden with Irish beef; which we bought in exchange for some of our sugar.

Bon-Airy is the Easternmost of the Dutch Islands, and is the largest of the three, though not the most considerable. The middle of the island is laid down in lat. 12 d. 16 m. It is about 20 leagues from the main, and 9 or 10 from Querisao, and is accounted 16 or 17 leagues round. The road is on the S. W. side, near the middle of the island; where there is a pretty deep bay runs in. Ships that come from the eastward luff up close to the Eastern shore:

and let go their anchor in 60 fathom water, within half a cable's length of the shore. But at the same time they must be ready with a boat to carry a hawser or rope, and make it fast ashore; otherwise, when the land-wind comes in the night, the ship would drive off to sea again; for the ground is so steep, that no anchor can hold if once it starts. About half a mile to the westward of this anchoring place there is a small low island, and a channel between it and the main island.

The houses are about half a mile within land, right in the road: there is a Governour lives here, a deputy to the Governour of Querisao, and 7 or 8 soldiers, with 5 or 6 families of Indians. There is no fort; and the soldiers in peaceable times have little to do but to eat and sleep, for they never watch, but in time of war. The Indians are husband-men, and plant maize and guinea corn, and some yams, and potatoes: but their chiefest business is about cattle; for this island is plentifully stocked with goats: and they send great quantities every year in salt to Querisao. There are some horses, and bulls and cows; but I never saw any sheep, though I have been all over the island. The South side is plain low land, and there are several sorts of trees, but none very large. There is a small spring of water by the houses, which serves the inhabitants, though it is blackish. At the West end of the island there is a good spring of fresh water, and 3 or 4 Indian families live there, but no water nor houses at any other place. On the South side near the East end, is a good salt-pond, where Dutch sloops come for salt.

From Bon-Airy we went to the Isle of Aves, or birds; so called from its great plenty of birds, as men-of-war and boobies; but especially boobies. The booby is a waterfowl, somewhat less than a hen, of a light grayish colour. I observed the boobies of this island to be whiter than others. This bird hath a strong bill, longer and bigger than a crow's, and broader at the end: her feet are flat like a duck's feet. It is a very simple creature, and will hardly go out of a man's way. In other places they build their nests on the ground, but here they build on trees; which I never saw any where else; though I have seen of them in a great many places. Their flesh is black and eats fishy, but are often eaten by the privateers. Their numbers have been much lessened by the French fleet, which was lost here, as I shall give an account.

The man-of-war (as it is called by the English) is about the bigness of a kite, and in shape like it, but black; and the neck is red. It lives on fish, yet never lights on the water, but soars aloft like a kite, and when it sees its prey, it flies down head foremost to the water's edge, very swiftly takes its prey out of the sea with its bill, and immediately mounts again as swiftly; and never touching the water with his bill. His wings are very long, his feet are like other land fowl, and he builds on trees, where he finds any; but where they are wanting, on the ground.

This island Aves lies about 8 or 9 leagues to the Eastward of the island Bon-Airy, about 14 or 15 leagues from the main, and about the lat. of 11 d. 45 m. North. It is but small, not above 4 mile in length, and towards the East end not half a mile broad. On the North side it is low land, commonly overflown with the tide; but on the South side there is a great rocky bank of coral thrown up by the sea. The West end is, for near a mile space, plain even savannah land, without any trees. There are 2 or 3 wells dug by privateers, who often frequent this island, because there is a good harbour about the middle of it on the North side, where they may conveniently careen. The reef, or bank of rocks, on which the French fleet was lost, as I mentioned above, runs along from the East end to the Northward about 3 miles, then trends away to the Westward, making as it were a half-moon. This reef breaks off all the sea, and there is good riding in even sandy ground to the Westward of it. There are 2 or 3 small low sandy keys, or islands, within this reef, about 3 miles from the main island.

The Count d'Estre lost his fleet here in this manner. Coming from the Eastward, he fell in on the back of the reef, and fired guns to give warning to the rest of his fleet: but they supposing their admiral was engaged with enemies, hoisted up their topsails, and crowded all the sails they could make, and ran full sail ashore after him; all within half a mile of each other. For his light being in the main-top was an unhappy beacon for them to follow; and there escaped but one kings-ship, and one privateer. The ships continued whole all day, and the men had time enough, most of them, to get ashore, yet many perished in the wreck: and many of those that got safe on the island, for want of being accustomed to such hardships, died like rotten sheep. But the privateers who had been used to such accidents lived merrily, from whom I had this relation: and they told me, that if they had gone to Jamaica with 30 *l.* a man in their pockets, they could not have enjoyed themselves more: for they kept in a gang by themselves, and watched when the ships broke, to get the goods that came from them; and though much was staved against the rocks, yet abundance of wine and brandy floated over the reef, where the privateers waited to take it up. They lived here about 3 weeks, waiting an opportunity to transport themselves back again to Hispaniola; in all which time they were never without 2 or 3 hogsheads of wine and brandy in their tents, and barrels of beef and pork; which they could live on without bread well enough, though the new-comers out of France could not. There were about forty Frenchmen on board in one of the ships where there was good store of liquor, till the after part of her broke away and floated over the reef, and was carried away to sea, with all the men drinking and singing, who being in drink, did not mind the danger, but were never heard of afterwards.

Excerpt from

A MINSTREL IN
FRANCE

by

HARRY LAUDER

Sometimes, but not often, we passed troops marching along the road. They swung along. They marched easily, with the stride that could carry them furthest with the least effort. They did not look much like the troops I used to see in London. They did not have the snap of the Coldstream Guards, marching through Green Park in the old days. But they looked like business and like war. They looked like men who had a job of work to do and meant to see it through.

They had discipline, those laddies, but it was not the old, stiff discipline of the old army. That is a thing of a day that is dead and gone. Now, as we passed along the side of the road that marching troops always leave clear, there was always a series of hails for me.

"Hello, Harry!" I would hear.

And I would look back, and see grinning Tommies waving their hands to me. It was a flattering experience, I can tell you, to be recognized like that along that road. It was like running into old friends in a strange town where you have come thinking you know no one at all.

We were about thirty miles out of Boulogne when there was a sudden explosion underneath the car, followed by a sibilant sound that I knew only too well.

"Hello – a puncture!" said Godfrey, and smiled as he turned around. We drew up to the side of the road, and both chauffeurs jumped out and went to work on the recalcitrant tire. The rest of us sat still, and gazed around us at the fields. I was glad to have a chance to look quietly about. The fields stretched out, all emerald green, in all directions to the distant horizon, sapphire blue that glorious morning. And in the fields, here and there, were the bent, stooped figures of old men and women. They were carrying on, quietly. Husbands and sons and brothers had gone to war; all the young men of France had gone. These were left, and they were seeing to the performance of the endless cycle of duty. France would survive; the Hun could not crush her. Here was a spirit made manifest – a spirit different in degree but not in kind from the spirit of my ain Britain. It brought a lump into my throat to see them, the old men and the women, going so patiently and quietly about their tasks.

It was very quiet. Faint sounds came to us; there was a distant rumbling, like the muttering of thunder on a summer's night, when the day has been hot and there are low, black clouds lying against the horizon, with the flashes of the lightning playing through them. But that I had come already not to heed, though I knew full well, by now, what it was and what it meant. For a little space the busy road had become clear; there was a long break in the traffic.

I turned to Adam and to Captain Godfrey.

"I'm thinking here's a fine chance for a bit of a rehearsal in the open air," I said. "I'm not used to singing so – mayhap it would be well to try my voice and see will it carry as it should."

"Right oh!" said Godfrey.

And so we dug Johnson out from his snug barricade of cigarettes, that hid him as an emplacement hides a gun, and we unstrapped my wee piano, and set it up in the road. Johnson tried the piano, and then we began.

I think I never sang with less restraint in all my life than I did that quiet morning on the Boulogne road. I raised my voice and let it have its will. And I felt my spirits rising with the lilt of the melody. My voice rang out, full and free, and it must have carried far and wide across the fields.

My audience was small at first – Captain Godfrey, Hogge, Adam, and the two chauffeurs, working away, and having more trouble with the tire than they had thought at first they would – which is the way of tires, as every man knows who owns a car. But as they heard my songs the old men and women in the fields straightened up to listen. They stood wondering, at first, and then, slowly, they gave over their work for a space, and came to gather round me and to listen.

It must have seemed strange to them! Indeed, it must have seemed strange to anyone had they seen and heard me! There I was, with Johnson at my piano, like some wayside tinker setting up his cart and working at his trade! But I did not care for appearances – not a whit. For the moment I was care free, a wandering minstrel, like some troubadour of old, care free and happy in my song. I forgot the black shadow under which we all lay in that smiling land, the black shadow of war in which I sang.

It delighted me to see those old peasants and to study their faces, and to try to win them with my song. They could not understand a word I sang, and yet I saw the smiles breaking out over their wrinkled faces, and it made me proud and happy. For it was plain that I was reaching them – that I was able to throw a bridge over the gap of a strange tongue and an alien race. When I had done and it was plain I meant to sing no more they clapped me.

"There's a hand for you, Harry," said Adam. "Aye – and I'm proud of it!" I told him for reply.

I was almost sorry when I saw that the two chauffeurs had finished their repairs and were ready to go on. But I told them to lash the piano back in its place, and Johnson prepared to climb gingerly back among his cigarettes. But just then something happened that I had not expected.

There was a turn in the road just beyond us that hid its continuation from us. And around the bend now there came a company of soldiers. Not neat and well-appointed soldiers these. Ah, no! They were fresh from the trenches, on their way back to rest. The mud and grime of the trenches were upon them. They were tired and weary, and they carried all their accoutrements and packs with them. Their boots were heavy with mud. And they looked bad, and many of them shaky.

Most of these men, Godfrey told me after a glance at them, had been ordered back to hospital for minor ailments. They were able to march, but not much more.

They were the first men I had seen in such a case. They looked bad enough, but Godfrey said they were happy enough. Some of them would get leave for Blighty, and be home, in a few days, to see their families and their girls. And they came swinging along in fine style, sick and tired as they were, for the thought of where they were going cheered them and helped to keep them going.

They eyed me very curiously as they came along, those sick laddies. They couldn't seem to understand what I was doing there, but their discipline held them. They were in charge of a young lieutenant with one star – a second lieutenant. I learned later that he was a long way from being a well man himself. So I stopped him. "Would your men like to hear a few songs, lieutenant?" I asked him.

He hesitated. He didn't quite understand, and he wasn't a bit sure what his duty was in the circumstances. He glanced at Godfrey, and Godfrey smiled at him as if in encouragement.

"It's very good of you, I'm sure," he said, slowly. "Fall out!"

So the men fell out, and squatted there, along the wayside. At once discipline was relaxed. Their faces were a study as the wee piano was set up again, and Johnson, in uniform, of course sat down and tried a chord or two. And then suddenly something happened that broke the ice. Just as I stood up to sing a loud voice broke the silence.

"Lor' love us!" one of the men cried, "if it ain't old 'Arry Lauder!"

There was a stir of interest at once. I spotted the owner of the voice. It was a shriveled up little chap, with a weazened face that looked like a sun-dried apple. He was showing all his teeth in a grin at me, and he was a typical little cockney of the sort all Londoners know well.

"Go it, 'Arry!" he shouted, shrilly. "Many's the time h' I've 'eard you at the old Shoreditch!"

So I went it as well as I could, and I never did have a more appreciative audience. My little cockney friend seemed to take a particular personal pride in me. I think he thought he had found me, and that he was, in an odd way, responsible for my success with his mates. And so he was especially glad when they cheered me and thanked me as they did.

My concert didn't last long, for we had to be getting on, and the company of sick men had just so much time, too, to reach their destination – Boulogne, whence we had set out. When it was over I said good-by to the men, and shook hands with particular warmth with the little cockney. It wasn't every day I was likely to meet a man who had often heard me at the old Shoreditch! After we had stowed Johnson and the piano away again, with a few less cigarettes, now, to get in Johnson's way, we started, and as long as we were in sight the little cockney and I were waving to one another.

We hope you enjoyed Walter Noble Burns's *A Year With A Whaler*. This book was entirely redesigned from an original edition, published in 1913, although spelling and vernacular were maintained. For additional information and other interesting historical memoirs from 1500 Books visit our web site at www.1500Books.com